WHAT HUSBANDS WANT AND WHAT WIVES 'REALLY' WANT

What Men [Husbands] Want From Their Women [Wives] & What Women [Wives] 'Really' Want From Their Men [Husbands]

MICHAEL HUTTON-WOOD

HWP

WARNING:

WOMAN/WIFE: BUY THIS BOOK FOR HIM!

MAN/HUSBAND: BUY THIS BOOK FOR HER!)

Unless otherwise indicated, all scriptural references are taken from the King James Version of the Bible

**WHAT HUSBANDS WANT
AND WHAT WIVES 'REALLY' WANT**

ISBN 978-0-9562541-6-0

Copyright © JUNE 2011 by Michael Hutton-Wood

Hutton-Wood publications

In the UK write to:

Michael Hutton-Wood Ministries

P. O. Box 1226, Croydon. CR9 6DG.

Or in the UK

Call: Tel. 020 8689 6010; 07956 815 714

Outside the UK call: +44 20 8689 6010; +44 7956 815 714

Or contact:

WEBSITE: www.houseofjudah.org.uk

Email: michaelhutton-wood@fsmail.net

houseofjudah@ymail.com

leadersfactoryinternational@yahoo.com

Published & distributed by: Michael Hutton-Wood Ministries
(Incorporating Hutton-Wood World Outreach Ministries)
All rights reserved under international copyright law.
Written permission must be secured from the publisher to use or reproduce any part of this book.

Printed in the United Kingdom

THE MANDATE:

'...SET IN ORDER THE THINGS THAT ARE OUT OF ORDER AND RAISE AND APPOINT LEADERS IN EVERY CITY.' - Titus 1:5

MICHAEL HUTTON-WOOD MINISTRIES

RELEASING POTENTIAL

- MAXIMIZING DESTINY

HOUSE OF JUDAH (PRAISE) MINISTRIES

&

LEADERS FACTORY INTERNATIONAL

RAISING GENERATIONAL LEADERS

- IMPACTING NATIONS

SIMPA: SCEPTRE INTERNATIONAL MINISTERS & PASTORS ASSOCIATION

EQUIPPING, EMPOWERING, COACHING, MENTORING AND PROVIDING COVERING FOR PASTORS, MINISTERS AND LEADERS ACROSS THE NATIONS!

CONTENTS

Dedication & Acknowledgements ... 6

Introduction ... 8

Part One

Chapter One: What Is Marriage? 40 Facts About Marriage ... 22

Chapter Two: 75 Secrets For Keeping Your Marriage Alive & Well (75 Keys To Staying Married) ... 42

Section One: Fighting For Your Marriage Through Spiritual Warfare

Section Two: Understanding And Engaging The Force Of Wisdom

Section Three: Communication – The Great Priority

Section Four: Romance And General Matters

Section Five: Money Matters

Section Six: Sexual Matters

Section Seven: Living A Life Of Gratitude, Thankfulness, Praise And Joyfulness

Part Two

(What Men [Husbands] Want From Their Women [Wives] & What Women [Wives] 'Really' Want From Their Men [Husbands]) ... 86

Chapter Three: What Women 'Really' Want [What Your Wife Really Wants] ... 88

Chapter Four: What Men Want [What Your Husband Wants] ... 124

Chapter Five: Women Become Men When Men Stop Being Men ... 154
  Includes: The Five Roles Of Every Man

Exercise For Both Husband & Wife [Relationship Indicator Charts] ... 186

Chillax: Funny Jokes About Marriage – Laugh Your Head Off ... 190

DEDICATION & ACKNOWLEDGEMENTS

First of all, to the Author of the institution of marriage, God our Father, Jesus, for not holding back but giving of yourself till you became a gift to give us richly **all things to enjoy and not endure** including principles for fulfilling marriages from your Word (1 Timothy 6:17), and the Holy Spirit our Illuminator and Enlightener, I GIVE YOU THANKS!

Secondly: To those whose marriages inspired us, mentors whose words of wisdom made us wiser, to credible teachers who taught us the right steps to take and to those numerous writers on this subject whose resource materials including books, DVDs CDs we gleaned what we know and practice now and whose seminars we attended and has made us wiser than our teachers, the Lord bless you for showing us the right way as you directed us to the following scriptures:

Proverbs 22:28-29, 'Remove not the ancient landmark, which thy fathers have set. Seest thou a man diligent in his business? he shall stand before kings; he shall not stand before mean men.'

Indeed, King Solomon was right when he said in Ecclesiastes 1:9-11, 'The thing that hath been, it is that which shall be; and that which is done is that which shall be done: and there is no new thing under the sun. Is there any thing whereof it may be said, See, this is new? it hath been already of old time, which was before us. There is no remembrance of former things; neither shall there be any remembrance of things that are to come with those that shall come after.

Thank God for teachers:

Isaiah 30:20-21, 'And though the Lord give you the bread of adversity, and the water of affliction, yet shall not thy teachers be removed into a corner any more, but thine eyes shall see thy teachers: And thine ears shall hear a word behind thee, saying, This is the way, walk ye in it, when ye turn to the right hand, and when ye turn to the left.'

May God continue to magnify your efforts. Shalom!

INTRODUCTION

As I said in the introduction to my book: "TAKING THE STRUGGLE OUT OF MINISTRY", 'EMBARKING ON ANY MINISTRY-RELATED ENTERPRISE WITHOUT UNDERSTANDING ITS DYNAMICS, REQUIREMENTS AND WHAT MAKES THINGS HAPPEN WITHOUT TOILING, SWEATING NEEDLESSLY OR STRUGGLE IS EQUIVALENT TO MADNESS.'

In the same way, entering marriage **without** a deep understanding of its intricacies, i.e. what it is, what it requires, getting the relevant information and knowledge backed by wisdom, revelation, insight and power from on High, what's involved, the principles that makes it work and what makes it fail or without adequate preparation is equivalent to madness of the highest order. The following two quotes that most people attribute to Albert Einstein depicts this clearly: "Insanity is doing the same thing over and over again but expecting different results."

'We cannot solve our problems with the same thinking we used when we created them.'

As my father in the Lord said: Nobody will call you mad if only you discover your madness before anybody else does! You are only called mad because somebody else discovered your madness before you did! Nobody will ever have the audacity to call you ignorant or a failure at anything including your marriage if only you discover your ignorance of the right marriage keys which leads to failure and engage the truth before anybody else does! You are only called mad, ignorant or a failure because somebody else discovered your madness before you did!

IT IS INDEED MADNESS TO ENTER A LIFELONG INSTITUTION LIKE MARRIAGE KNOWING NOTHING OR NEXT TO NOTHING ABOUT IT OR UNDERSTANDING WHAT IT REALLY IS OR BASED ON ASSUMPTIONS, OR HEARSAY. However, if you take quality time to find out what it is, what you must do, and do it, the right button to press, and press it, the right step to take, and take it, God is committed to empower you to make it work. You are only called mad, ignorant or a failure because somebody else discovered your madness or ignorance before you did. King Solomon advised that in all our getting we should get wisdom and understanding so we don't become casualties in any area of our lives. So, we will begin by finding out through studying, knowing and getting understanding of what marriage is. That is wisdom! Wisdom is, knowing the right thing to learn, right thing to think, right thing to say and right thing to do at the right time, in the right way, with the right tone, in the right place, with the right attitude and with the right motive. Happiness both in life and in marriage is always there within reach, no matter how long it lasts. Let's enjoy life and don't live a complicated life. Life is too short. Work at your marriage as if it was your first day. Forgive as soon as possible. Love without boundaries. Laugh without control and never stop smiling.

REMEMBER:

- THERE ARE NO HARD PLACES; THERE ARE ONLY HARD PEOPLE!

- THERE IS NO MOUNTAIN ANYWHERE IN YOUR MARRIAGE; EVERYBODY'S IGNORANCE OF THE RIGHT MARRIAGE KEYS OR PRINCIPLES IS WHAT THEY LABEL A MOUNTAIN!

- SO: IN ALL YOUR GETTING, GET UNDERSTANDING: WHY?

At The root of everything outstanding is understanding!

IF YOU WANT TO BECOME OUTSTANDING IN YOUR MARRIAGE THEN FIRST GO FOR UNDERSTANDING.

UNDERSTANDING TAKES EVERY TOIL AND STRUGGLE OUT OF EVERY VENTURE INCLUDING MARRIAGE RELATIONSHIPS AND EMPOWERS YOU TO STAND OUT AND BECOME THE STANDARD.

Marriage is not a relegation to a life of struggles, endless suffering or tolerating each other but a journey of bliss and fulfilment. (John 10:10) So, get your instructions from Source before stepping out. Marriage is not a business transaction between two people or a game of pool, chess, monopoly or snakes and ladders but about people's destinies so do not treat it like one. Marriage is not a journey of trial and error. It's not guess work. Marriage begins with discovering from Source who you are supposed to fulfil DESTINY with [That is the key word – DESTINY – Marriage is about destiny].

WHO YOU MARRY IS NOT DECIDED – IT IS DISCOVERED!

WHO YOU MARRY IS NOT DECIDED OR DETERMINED BY YOU BUT BY DESTINY BECAUSE IT'S ALL ABOUT DESTINY FULFILMENT. Marrying the person of your choice without consultation with your POTTER is like the clay telling the potter what they want to be and is equivalent to taking on a suicidal mission. You won't fulfil destiny if you marry the wrong person. **SUBJECT YOUR HUMANITY AND CREATIVITY TO DIVINITY FOR APPROVAL SO YOU HAVE THE BLESSING ON IT!**

So find out from Source first His intention for you (Jeremiah 1:5-10; Hebrews 10:7; Psalm 40:7) because you are first and foremost here to fulfil His plan for you [in the volume of the books, what is written of you] and in that plan is an appointed person that will stand with you and you with them to fulfil destiny – so that is Number One. Then it must be initiated and motivated by love [Agape, Phileo, Storge, Eros - 1 Peter 3; 1 Corinthians 13] backed by adequate and relevant knowledge, understanding, devotion, diligence, selflessness, adequate preparation, determination, discipline, sacrifice and continuous application of wisdom to make it work before and throughout the marriage. Reason being: **IN LIFE YOU ARE EITHER BUILDING ON PRINCIPLES OR RUBBLES!**

YOU ARE EITHER BUILDING A LIBRARY OR A MORTUARY WITHOUT KNOWING! With the disciplined practice of the above will come grace, abilities, provision, endowments, confidence, boldness, manpower, resources, accuracy and precision in activating spiritual gifts, guidance, protection, financial provision, God's presence, weight, power and authority backing the things you do and words you speak and utter, confirmed with signs and wonders, activation of the angelic ministry, effectiveness, efficiency, success and undeniable results/proofs both in your marriage and your calling in life enabling you to fulfil destiny in a grand style without heartaches.

CRITERIA: 'All you need to do is learn of me (Joshua 1:8)' and from the reliable and credible resource materials like this book, fathers, credible mentors who have obtained what you desire to obtain both in your marriage and overall destiny, so you end up with a colourful marriage, children of destiny and complete fulfilment.

IT TAKES FATHERS TO FATHER YOU TO GROW FEATHERS TO FLY AND GO FURTHER THAN THEY HAVE GONE!

JUST AS: THERE IS NO FUTURE IN ANY JOB BUT RATHER IN THE ONE WHO HOLDS THE JOB, IN THE SAME WAY THERE IS NO FUTURE IN ANY MARRIAGE BUT RATHER IN THE ONES IN THE MARRIAGE – WHAT THEY KNOW AND DO – SO, IT'S NOT IN THE MARRIAGE – IT'S IN WHO IS IN THE MARRAGE i.e. THE PEOPLE IN IT AND WHAT THEY KNOW AND DO WITH THE MARRIAGE – THE

INSTITUTION!

UNDERSTANDING MAKES EVERYTHING OUTSTANDING!

IT'S NOT IN THE KNOWING - IT'S IN THE EXECUTION!

IT'S NOT IN JUST KNOWING WHAT TO DO BUT IN THE EXECUTION OF WHAT IS KNOWN AND UNDERSTOOD!

Your not seeing change is not because what you're doing is wrong; it's because you're not doing enough what is right.

That's why this book has been written. APPLYING AND LIVING BY THE CONTENTS OF THIS BOOK WILL TAKE THE SWEATING, TOILING, FRUSTRATION, FIGHTING AND STRUGGLE OUT OF YOUR MARRIAGE PERMANENTLY AND FOR THOSE STARTING NOW, I PROPHESY THAT BY BEING ADDICTED TO ENGAGING THESE TRUTHS, YOU WILL NEVER SWEAT ONCE!!

SAY A LOUD AMEN!

NOBODY WILL CALL YOU MAD IF ONLY YOU DISCOVER YOUR MADNESS BEFORE ANYBODY ELSE DOES!

YOU ARE ONLY CALLED MAD BECAUSE SOMEBODY ELSE DISCOVERED IT BEFORE YOU DID!

- Bishop David Oyedepo

THERE ARE NO HARD PLACES; THERE ARE ONLY HARD PEOPLE!

THERE IS NO MOUNTAIN ANYWHERE IN YOUR MARRIAGE; EVERYBODY'S IGNORANCE OF MARRIAGE KEYS IS WHAT THEY LABEL A MOUNTAIN!

A LABEL IS ONLY A LABEL; NOT THE REAL THING - YOU CAN CHANGE IT!

IT IS NOT YOUR PARTNER - IT IS YOUR PARTNERSHIP WITH IGNORANCE!

IT IS NOT YOUR PARTNER'S FAULT – IT IS YOUR FAULTY INFORMATION AND PRACTICE BASE!

YOU DON'T CALL SOMETHING OR SOMEONE HARD IF YOU KNOW WHAT SOFTENS IT OR THEM!

YOU DON'T FAIL AT MARRIAGE BECAUSE YOU DON'T KNOW ANYTHING – YOU FAIL AT MARRIAGE BECAUSE YOU DON'T KNOW ENOUGH OF WHAT IT TAKES TO MAKE IT WORK!

IF I FIND THE RIGHT BUTTON TO PRESS ON ANY ISSUE AND I PRESS IT, IT'S NO LONGER DIFFICULT - IS IT!

TRUTHS YOU MUST KNOW ABOUT MARRIAGE

- Marriage is an institution created by God.

- MARRIAGE IS A PERFECT INSTITUTION CREATED BY A PERFECT GOD, ENTERED INTO BY TWO IMPERFECT PEOPLE, MAKING PERFECT WELL-INTENDED VOWS FROM IMPERFECT LIPS TO EACH OTHER WHO ARE IMPERFECT [i.e. AN IMPERFECT PERSON] BEFORE A PERFECT GOD IN AN IMPERFECT ENVIRONMENT SURROUNDED BY IMPERFECT WITNESSES ABOUT TO LIVE TOGETHER IN AN IMPERFECT HOME HENCE THE NEED FOR THOSE TWO IMPERFECT PEOPLE TO BE ADDICTED TO, EMBRACE, USE, ENGAGE, AND BE GUIDED BY GOD'S PERFECT WORD TO BECOME THE PERFECT WORD IN THIS PERFECT INSTITUTION THEY'VE ENTERED INTO.

- Marriage is an institution you enter into not to change it, but to abide by its rules so you can benefit from what it has to offer you. So when you enter an institution like the above mentioned, you submit to the institution and the laws that govern it so you can get from it all that you went there for. You don't go there and try to change it to suit your purposes. Similarly, the Bible describes the institution of marriage as one that must be greatly and highly esteemed and respected. It is to be seen as most important, i.e. the institution - not the people in it.

- Marriage is a perfect institution for scripture says every good and perfect gift comes from above. (James 1:17)

- So Marriage itself is a perfect institution entered into by two imperfect people, committing themselves to this perfect institution by making perfect vows from imperfect lips. Only God can make this work.

- So, Marriage is two imperfect people, committing themselves to a perfect institution by making perfect vows such as, 'I will never leave you, till death would we part, for better or worse, [for better and better Proverbs 4:18] I'll be there in sickness or in health etc.' but this perfect well-intended vow is coming from imperfect lips hence the need for God's perfect word.

- SO MARRIAGE IS PERFECT, IT IS CONSTANT, IT DOES NOT CHANGE; IT IS THE PEOPLE IN IT THAT ARE NOT PERFECT AND ARE CHANGING. SO COMMIT YOURSELF TO SOMETHING THAT DOES NOT CHANGE AND NO MATTER HOW YOU CHANGE, THE THING WILL REMAIN THE SAME FOR YOU. As you live with each other you will discover changes in each of you, in other words you will not remain the same. Both of you will not remain the same forever. Man, the pretty lady you marry today at her age now will not be the one you will live with, in your house. She will be changing all the time and so will you.

- YOU DON'T LIVE DAY-TO-DAY WITH THE ONE YOU MARRIED.

PART ONE

Chapter One

WHAT AT ALL IS MARRIAGE?

WHERE PURPOSE IS UNKNOWN - ABUSE IS INEVITABLE!

Nobody will call you mad if only you discover your madness before anybody else does! You are only called mad because somebody else discovered it before you did! Nobody will ever have the audacity to call you ignorant or a failure at anything including your marriage if only you discover your ignorance of the right marriage keys which leads to failure and engage them before anybody else does! You are only called mad, ignorant or a failure because somebody else discovered it before you did! If you take quality time to find out what it is, what you must do, and do it, the right button to press, and press it, the right step to take, and take it, God is committed to empower you to make it work. You are only called mad, ignorant or a failure because somebody else discovered your madness or ignorance before you did. King Solomon said in all our getting we should get wisdom and understanding so we don't become casualties in any area of our lives. So, we will begin by finding out through studying, knowing and getting understanding of what marriage is. That is wisdom! Wisdom is, knowing the right thing to learn, right thing to think, right thing to say and right thing to do at the right time, in the right way, with the right tone, in the right place, with the right attitude and with the right motive.

Happiness both in life and in marriage is always there within reach, no matter how long it lasts. Let's enjoy life and don't live a complicated life. Life is too short. Work at your marriage as if it was your first day. Forgive as soon as possible. Love without boundaries. Laugh without control and never stop smiling.

REMEMBER:

- THERE ARE NO HARD PLACES; THERE ARE ONLY HARD PEOPLE!

- THERE IS NO MOUNTAIN ANYWHERE IN YOUR MARRIAGE; EVERYBODY'S IGNORANCE OF THE RIGHT MARRIAGE KEYS OR PRINCIPLES IS WHAT THEY LABEL A MOUNTAIN!

STONE

TWO FRIENDS WERE WALKING THROUGH THE DESERT. DURING SOME POINT OF THE JOURNEY, THEY HAD AN ARGUMENT; AND ONE FRIEND SLAPPED THE OTHER ONE IN THE FACE. THE ONE WHO GOT SLAPPED WAS HURT, BUT WITHOUT SAYING ANYTHING, WROTE IN THE SAND, 'TODAY MY BEST FRIEND SLAPPED ME IN THE FACE.'

THEY KEPT ON WALKING, UNTIL THEY FOUND AN OASIS, WHERE THEY DECIDED TO TAKE A BATH. THE ONE WHO HAD BEEN SLAPPED GOT STUCK IN THE MIRE AND STARTED DROWNING, BUT THE FRIEND SAVED HIM. AFTER HE RECOVERED FROM THE NEAR DROWNING, HE WROTE ON A STONE: 'TODAY MY BEST FRIEND SAVED MY LIFE.' THE FRIEND WHO HAD SLAPPED AND SAVED HIS BEST FRIEND ASKED HIM, 'AFTER I HURT YOU, YOU WROTE IN THE SAND AND NOW, YOU WRITE ON A STONE, WHY?'

THE FRIEND REPLIED: 'WHEN SOMEONE HURTS US, WE SHOULD WRITE IT DOWN IN SAND, WHERE WINDS OF FORGIVENESS CAN ERASE IT AWAY. BUT, WHEN SOMEONE DOES SOMETHING GOOD FOR US, WE MUST ENGRAVE IT IN STONE WHERE NO WIND CAN EVER ERASE IT.'

LEARN TO WRITE YOUR HURTS IN THE SAND AND TO CARVE YOUR BENEFITS IN STONE. THEY SAY: IT TAKES A MINUTE TO FIND A SPECIAL PERSON, AN HOUR TO APPRECIATE THEM, A DAY TO LOVE THEM, BUT THEN, AN ENTIRE LIFE TO FORGET THEM. TAKE THE TIME TO LIVE! DO NOT VALUE THE THINGS YOU HAVE IN YOUR LIFE, BUT VALUE <u>WHO</u> YOU HAVE KNOWN IN YOUR LIFE!

FOOLS BELIEVE IN LUCK; THE WISE BELIEVE IN THE LAW OF CAUSE AND EFFECT!

ALWAYS REMEMBER: IT DOESN'T TAKE TIME – IT TAKES TRUTH! "And in thy majesty ride prosperously because of truth and meekness and righteousness; and thy right hand shall teach thee terrible things." - Psalm 45:4

40 FACTS ABOUT MARRIAGE:

1. **Marriage: Definition** – As defined by the manual for living (God's Infallible, Unchanging Word – The Holy Bible), it is two people of the opposite sex brought together by God as part of the divine will and purpose of God to live out their lives on this earth based on the teachings of the Holy Scriptures

(The Bible).

2. Marriage is the joining together in holy matrimony of a man and a woman who are in love with each other, are convinced they are meant for each other with the intention of building a home together and for the purpose of fulfilling destiny together until death do they part. A healthy "house" and a healthy home is the key to both a healthy church and a healthy society.

3. The marriage union is the most intimate of all human relationships. For believers it is a union in the Lord. This covenanted union is initiated by God as a provision for the fulfilment, continuation, and edification of mankind which culminates in strong families who then produce strong churches. We all are products of our families, directly as well as indirectly.

4. Marriage is a FOREVER!

5. Marriage is a lifetime commitment.

6. Marriage means that everything is shared.

7. Marriage involves being with the same person for long periods of time.

8. Marriage is something like a big amplifier revealing what both of you never knew about each other.

9. Marriage is like a precious gem.

10. Marriage requires Unconditional love.

11. Marriage provides opportunities for both of you to accomplish a whole lot more [Getting more for your efforts] because two are better than one. Ecclesiastes 4:9, 'Two are better than one; because they have a good reward for their labour.'

12. Marriage provides warmth, confidence, stability and consistency.

13. Marriage involves being positively locked in with a single person, giving up a great deal of freedom and having to consult on most issues if not all.

14. Marriage involves your having to work to maintain and build your human qualities.

15. Marriage is God's idea, not just a good idea. It is only a good idea because it is GOD's idea.

16. Marriage is honourable. Hebrews 13:4 says, 'Marriage is honourable in all, and the bed undefiled: but whoremongers and adulterers God will judge.'

The amplified version says, 'Let marriage be held in honour (esteemed worthy, precious, of great price and especially dear in all things.'

So, it is marriage that is honourable not the people in it. The basic cause of failure in marriage is when people fail to recognize the fact that marriage is honourable not the people in it but marriage itself.

17. **Marriage is an institution.** It is a BLESSED and PERFECT institution and a thing practised on this earth only (Matthew 22:30; Mark 12:25; Luke 20:34-35). For anyone to have a successful marriage they must understand what marriage really is from God's point of view since He instituted it in the first place. Remember, where purpose is unknown, abuse is inevitable. So, before you encounter the insurmountable, why not go to the Manufacturer and ask some questions which only He can answer! Ask Him to explain to you what He had in mind when He instituted marriage. Seeing it through His eyes will save you all the heartache and frustration that others have been plagued with as a result of ignorance. Marriage is a wonderful thing, and provided we understand it and are prepared to work at it using the prescribed manual, we can really enjoy it and experience lasting fulfilment.

'For he that wanders away from the paths of understanding shall remain in the congregation of then dead.' - Proverbs 21:16

REMEMBER: You are not of the dead, but of the

living. So, in all your getting, get understanding of this subject first before you enter this race which has the potential of being the next thing to heaven on earth which if clearly understood before entered into or a life of self-invited and self-inflicted imprisonment with hard labour for the ignorant and jokers. For Bible says in Proverbs 13:15, 'Good understanding giveth favour: but the way of transgressors [the ignorant] is hard.'

UNDERSTANDING MARRIAGE AS AN INSTITUTION

YOU NEED TO SEE MARRIAGE AS AN INSTITUTION THAT IS HONOURABLE – HIGHLY ESTEEMED, MOST RESPECTACLE.

Scripture says in Proverbs 4:7, 'Wisdom is the principal thing; therefore get wisdom: and with all thy getting get understanding.'

For anyone to have a successful marriage they must understand what marriage really is from God's point of view since He instituted it in the first place. Remember, where purpose is unknown, abuse is inevitable. So, before you encounter the insurmountable, why not go to the manufacturer and ask some questions which only He can answer; ask Him to explain to you what He had in mind when He instituted marriage. Seeing it through His eyes will save you all the heartache and frustration that others have been plagued with as a result of ignorance. I repeat: Marriage is a wonderful thing, and provided we understand it and are prepared to work at it, we will enjoy it and experience lasting fulfilment.

18. Marriage is an institution created by God.

19. MARRIAGE IS A PERFECT INSTITUTION CREATED BY A PERFECT GOD, ENTERED INTO BY TWO IMPERFECT PEOPLE, MAKING PERFECT WELL-INTENDED VOWS FROM IMPERFECT LIPS TO EACH OTHER WHO ARE IMPERFECT [i.e. AN IMPERFECT PERSON] BEFORE A PERFECT GOD IN AN IMPERFECT ENVIRONMENT SURROUNDED BY IMPERFECT WITNESSES ABOUT TO LIVE TOGETHER IN AN IMPERFECT HOME HENCE THE NEED FOR THOSE TWO IMPERFECT PEOPLE TO BE ADDICTED TO, EMBRACE, USE, ENGAGE, AND BE GUIDED BY GOD'S PERFECT WORD TO BECOME THE PERFECT WORD IN THIS PERFECT INSTITUTION THEY'VE ENTERED INTO.

Marriage is an institution you enter into not to change it, but to abide by its rules so you can benefit from what it has to offer you, to make you a better person, more effective and prominent, a master at what you do, to graduate with distinction, increase your salary scale, go into the world and make a great impact in life from what you discovered and applied and eventually recommend it to others.

An institution is something that is established, set, fixed and bigger than one person and it is established before you met it. It was established, instituted before you met it. The following universities and colleges are typical examples of what an institution is: Harvard, Yale, Moorhouse, Regents, Oral Roberts University, (USA) Oxford, Cambridge, Kings College, (UK) Covenant University & Landmark University (Nigeria) Central University College, (Ghana) etc.

So when you enter an institution like the above mentioned, you submit to the institution and the laws that govern it so you can get from it all that you went there for. You take time to discover the times for waking up, your daily schedule, time-table, where the offices and various faculties are located, etc. and you adapt until you graduate from that institution. You don't go there and try to change it to suit your purposes. Similarly, the Bible describes the institution of marriage as one that must be greatly and highly esteemed and respected. It is to be seen as most important, i.e. the institution - not the people in it.

The people in it or the people entering it must see this institution they are entering into as highly esteemed and most important. You submit to it. So, Marriage is a perfect institution for scripture says every good and perfect gift comes from above. (James 1:17)

20. So Marriage itself is a perfect institution entered into by two imperfect people, committing themselves to this perfect institution by making perfect vows from imperfect lips. Only God can make this work. That is why you need His manual for successful living containing the wisdom you need which is the principal thing. If you want to see the first imperfect person, look in the mirror. (Joshua 1:8; Proverbs 4:20-24; Psalm 1:1-3; Psalm 119:89-105, 130; Proverbs 4:7; Hebrews 4:12; Deuteronomy 28:1-14; James 1:23-25)

So, Marriage is two imperfect people, committing themselves to a perfect institution by making perfect vows such as, 'I will never leave you, till death would we part, for better or worse, [for better and better Proverbs 4:18] I'll be there in sickness or in health etc.' but this perfect well-intended vow is coming from imperfect lips.

21. SO MARRIAGE IS PERFECT, IT IS CONSTANT, IT DOES NOT CHANGE; IT IS THE PEOPLE IN IT THAT ARE NOT PERFECT AND ARE CHANGING. SO COMMIT YOURSELF TO SOMETHING THAT DOES NOT CHANGE AND NO MATTER HOW YOU CHANGE, THE THING WILL REMAIN THE SAME FOR YOU. As you live with each other you will discover changes in each of you, in other words you will not remain the same. Both of you will not remain the same forever. Man, the pretty lady you marry today at her age now will not be the one you will live with, in your house. She will be changing all the time and so will you.

YOU DON'T LIVE DAY-TO-DAY WITH THE ONE YOU MARRIED.

Why? Because, they are changing all the time, so are you. So, don't commit yourself to him/her per se but to the institution of marriage that is highly esteemed and must be most respected. Because, you will keep changing, your commitment should be to the institution of marriage so that despite the changes you may see in each other physically, biologically, the age process etc, you will still remain committed to the marriage. For instance, when you join an institution, like a factory, job, college or university, you conform to the set rules laid out there before you joined. You don't go and change the rules to suit your needs or wants or desires. You can make suggestions as to how things can get better but you don't rise up in defiance to change the laid down principles. Principles cannot be changed but methods can and in marriage like an institution, God has laid down certain principles which when you follow, you will get His kind of results.

Violating that will be detrimental to you. When someone upsets or annoys you on the job, you don't just leave that job neither do you resign because you notice that your boss's hair or contemporaries' hair is falling off or the one who sits next to you in the office is going bald, or his/her teeth is falling out or is losing their gorgeous looks, you don't resign from the job and say I am going to look for another job. If you even disagree with them you don't leave that job, you may not speak to them for a little while, but you sort yourself out later on and begin to speak again to each other and so is marriage; you work at relationships till you get it right. The reason why you sort yourselves out and stay on the job is because you consider the institution as more important than your personal feelings so both of you stay on the job.

Another example is when you are undertaking a course and pursuing a degree in an institution like a university and a lecturer or the vice chancellor or a fellow student upsets you real bad, you don't abandon your course or leave that university to look for another one because of that one person's behaviour. You may express your dissatisfaction but you wouldn't stop pursuing your destiny, your future because of that. So changing the institution is not the solution to the problem – just like getting married to someone else will not be the solution to the problem. That is why divorce courts are like taking paracetamol tablets to cure your chronic migraine. So your commitment to the marriage is your key to success. That is why we must make up our mind that no matter what my wife does to me or my husband does to me, he/she is tripping if they think I will resign because Resignation is divorce. It is not an option because I am not committed to him/her per se but the institution of marriage that I have committed myself to. So the factory does not break down because you quarrelled or were in disagreement with a work colleague. This is not your factory - it is bigger than you so you can't fire people from it. Your attitude should be, 'I don't care what you do to me - you can't get me to resign from you; since we have to work in this office or live and work together in this marriage we might just as well try and get along to make this thing work. Reason being - marriage belongs to God.'

Marriage is an institution - it is constant.

22. Remember, you can't fire anyone from a marriage; it is not yours - it belongs to God, so you can't fire the person. We have been making the people honourable whilst the people are changing forgetting that people in the marriage are changing but marriage itself is constant.

23. Success in marriage does not depend on spouses committing themselves to EACH OTHER as much as it does to their committing themselves to MARRIAGE, the unchanging institution that they have MUTUALLY entered into. Your commitment as long as you remain in that institution is to the institution and so is the marriage [institution]. So, no matter what happens, you are committed to what you committed your life to – the institution of marriage.

24. **It's not who you love but what you love – honour and esteem marriage itself.**

25. Marriage is a steady unchanging institution entered into by two people who are constantly changing as they grow and mature. Whenever you are entering marriage, commit yourself to the marriage, not the person, because people – everybody grows and change takes place. If you commit yourself to whoever you marry and think they will remain the same physically, you are deceived.

26. Marriage is bigger than the two people in it.

27. Marriage is two imperfect people committing themselves to a perfect institution, by making perfect vows from imperfect lips.

28. A Happy Marriage is No Accident – it is consciously and deliberately created through the manual, (the Word - Joshua 1:8) continuous nurturing and careful cultivation – you work at it by understanding and engaging what I call THE LOVE COMBINATION ANOINTING [COMBO].

29. Remember: **LOVE IS NOT JUST A FEELING, BUT A DISCIPLINE. IT IS A CHOICE. IT IS A DECISION.**

30. **IT TAKES ONLY A FEW MINUTES TO GET MARRIED! BUT BUILDING A MARRIAGE REQUIRES A LIFETIME.**

MANY SPEND MORE TIME, RESOURCES AND ENERGY DATING BEFORE MARRIAGE AND STOP DATING AFTER MARRIAGE WHEN IN ACTUAL FACT, DATING SHOULD HAVE CONTINUED AFTER THE WEDDING - in the context of marriage. I repeat: It takes only a few minutes to get married, but building a marriage requires a lifetime.

31. A GOOD MARRIAGE IS WHAT YOU MAKE IT. **Marriage is the next thing to heaven on earth or a hellish life imprisonment on earth with hard labour – you choose!** Deuteronomy 30:19, 'I call heaven and earth to record this day against you, that I have set before you life and death, blessing and cursing: therefore choose life, that both thou and thy seed may live:'

Joshua 24:15, 'And if it seem evil unto you to serve the LORD, choose you this day whom ye will serve; whether the gods which your fathers served that were on the other side of the flood, or the gods of the Amorites, in whose land ye dwell: but as for me and my house, we will serve the LORD.'

32. MARRIAGE INVOLVES HARD, SMART, CREATIVE, INNOVATIVE WORK USING THE APPOINTED MANUAL – THE BIBLE!

33. MARRIAGE REQUIRES UNENDING CREATIVITY, INNOVATIVENESS AND TAKING DELIGHTFUL INITITATIVES FOR EACH OTHER'S BENEFIT.

34. MARRIAGE IS NOT JUST GIVING 50/50 - IT IS ESSENTIALLY GIVING 100% OF ALL YOU ARE AND ALL YOU HAVE.

35. MARRIAGE IS NOT FOR BETTER OR WORSE BUT FOR BETTER AND BETTER AND BETTER AND BETTER.

PROOF: Ecclesiastes 4:9, 'Two are better than one; because they have a good reward for their labour.'

Psalm 115:14, 'The LORD shall increase you more and more, you and your children.'

Proverbs 4:18, 'But the path of the just is as the shining light, that shineth more and more unto the perfect day.'

36. It is very important for us to know that marriage is a mystery of two people becoming one. In God's concept of marriage, **two people alone make a home**. That's why God said in His Word: 'For this cause shall a man leave his father…and cleave to his wife….' **(Mark 10:7).**

37. A home is formed at the coming together of **ONLY TWO**, not more. 'When they are more than two, it becomes a house.' (Bishop Oyedepo) God's original design for marriage is for a man and a woman to come together in holy matrimony. **Two Alone Make a Home, Not More Than Two!**

38. The success or failure of your home should not

be left at the mercy of extended family members. 'What therefore God hath joined together, let no man put asunder.' **(Matthew 19:6)** It is not God's will that anything/anyone should put your home asunder, not even your in-laws.

39. The man is the principal figure in the family unit providing direction, guidance, vision, provision – all motivated by love.

40. Love is the master key and price a man pays for a glorious home.

Chapter Two

75 SECRETS FOR KEEPING YOUR MARRIAGE ALIVE AND WELL

[I.e. 75 KEYS TO STAYING MARRIED]

THIS CHAPTER CONTAINS SEVEN SECTIONS:

Section One: **Fighting For Your Marriage Through Spiritual Warfare**

Section Two: **Understanding And Engaging The Force Of Wisdom**

Section Three: **Communication – the Great Priority**

Section Four: **Romance And General Matters**

Section Five: **Money Matters**

Section Six: **Sexual Matters**

Section Seven: **Living A Life Of Gratitude, Thankfulness, Praise And Joyfulness**

SECTION ONE:

FIGHTING FOR YOUR MARRIAGE THROUGH SPIRITUAL WARFARE

1. YOU DON'T HAVE A SPECIAL PROBLEM IN YOUR MARRIAGE - YOU JUST HAD A SPECIAL IGNORANCE: Hosea 4:6, 'My people are destroyed for lack of knowledge: because thou hast rejected knowledge, I will also reject thee, that thou shalt be no priest to me: seeing thou hast forgotten the law of thy God, I will also forget thy children.'

2. STAY IN THE WORD, CEASELESS PRAYER AND PRAISE:

There is no mountain anywhere-everybody's ignorance is their mountain!

(John 1:1; Hebrews 11:1-6; 4:12; 1 Thessalonians 5:17; Psalm 34; 103)

3. LIFE DOES NOT GIVE YOU WHAT YOU

DESERVE - LIFE GIVES YOU WHAT YOU DEMAND!

SO, CONTEND AND POSSESS: Deuteronomy 2:24, 'Rise ye up, take your journey, and pass over the river Arnon: behold, I have given into thine hand Sihon the Amorite, king of Heshbon, and his land: begin to possess it, and contend with him in battle.'

4. POSSESS WITH PATIENCE:

Luke 21:19, 'In your patience possess ye your souls.'

5. FIGHT FOR YOUR MARRIAGE: Fight the good fight of faith..

LIFE IS NOT A PLAYGROUND – LIFE IS A BATTLEGROUND!

Ephesians 6:10-12, 'Finally, my brethren, be strong in the Lord, and in the power of his might. Put on the whole armour of God, that ye may be able to stand against the wiles of the devil. For we wrestle not against flesh and blood, but against principalities, against powers, against the rulers of the darkness of this world, against spiritual wickedness in high places.'

6. LIFE IS NOT A FUNFARE – LIFE IS A WARFARE:

2 Corinthians 10:4, '(For the weapons of our warfare are not carnal, but mighty through God to the pulling down of strong holds;)'

7. INVEST IN YOUR MARRIAGE! Your input determines your output! Joshua 1:8, 'This book of the law shall not depart out of thy mouth; but thou shalt meditate therein day and night, that thou mayest observe to do according to all that is written therein: for then thou shalt make thy way prosperous, and then thou shalt have good success.'

8. FIGHT THE GOOD FIGHT OF FAITH TO LAY HOLD ON WHAT IS YOURS: 1 Timothy 6:12, 'Fight the good fight of faith, lay hold on eternal life, whereunto thou art also called, and hast professed a good profession before many witnesses.'

9. TAKE WHAT IS YOURS BY FORCE: Matthew 11:12, 'And from the days of John the Baptist until now the kingdom of heaven suffereth violence, and the violent take it by force.'

10. PURSUE, OVERTAKE AND RECOVER ALL: 1 Samuel 30:8, 'And David inquired at the LORD, saying, Shall I pursue after this troop? shall I overtake them? And he answered him, Pursue: for thou shalt surely overtake them, and without fail recover all.'

SECTION TWO:

UNDERSTANDING AND ENGAGING THE FORCE OF WISDOM

11. IN ALL YOUR GETTING, GET WISDOM AND APPLY WISDOM - YOU WILL BE AMAZED AT WHAT IT DOES TO, FOR, WITH AND IN YOUR MARRIAGE:

WHAT IS WISDOM?

Why is it so crucial for my marriage?

I am so glad you asked this question:

In life you are either learning from mistakes or mentors. You receive wisdom from mentors. Observe them, learn from them and sow into their lives. Engaging the Law of Observation endows you with wisdom which is the Principal Raw Material for the Making of and the sustaining of a Great Marriage.

Matthew 13:54, 'And when he was come into his own country, he taught them in their synagogue, insomuch that they were astonished, and said, Whence hath this man this wisdom, and these mighty works?'

Matthew 7:24-28, 'Therefore whosoever heareth these sayings of mine, and doeth them, I will liken him unto a wise man, which built his house upon a rock: And the rain descended, and the floods came, and the winds blew, and beat upon that house; and it fell not: for it was founded upon a rock. And every one that heareth these sayings of mine, and doeth them not, shall be likened unto a foolish man, which built his house upon the sand: And the rain descended, and the floods came, and the winds blew, and beat upon that house; and it fell: and great was the fall of it. And it came to pass, when Jesus had ended these sayings, the people were astonished at his doctrine:'

Mark 6:2, 'And when the sabbath day was come, he began to teach in the synagogue: and many hearing him were astonished, saying, From whence hath this man these things? and what wisdom is this which is given unto him, that even such mighty works are wrought by his hands?'

Now let's examine:

VITAL TRUTHS ABOUT WISDOM AND CONTINUOUS LEARNING IN SUSTAINING YOUR MARRIAGE:

32 FACTS ABOUT WISDOM AND ITS BENEFITS:

1. Wisdom is the principal [first] thing you need. Proverbs 4:7-9, 'Wisdom is the principal thing; therefore get wisdom: and with all thy getting get understanding. Exalt her, and she shall promote thee: she shall bring thee to honour, when thou dost embrace her. She shall give to thine head an ornament of grace: a crown of glory shall she deliver to thee.'

2. You reign and rule by wisdom. Proverbs 8:15-16, 'By me kings reign, and princes decree justice. By me princes rule, and nobles, even all the judges of the earth.'

Just as flour is the principal raw material for making or baking cakes, so is wisdom for making great marriages and kings.

3. You must love and pursue wisdom. Proverbs 8:17, 'I love them that love me; and those that seek me early shall find me.'

4. Richness, honour, durable [lasting] riches and righteousness can only be found in the force of wisdom. Proverbs 8:18, 'Riches, and honour are with me; yea, durable riches and righteousness.'

5. Wisdom is the ability to make use of knowledge effectively. Wisdom demands that you hear and

apply.

6. Wisdom is not just the ability to think or the engagement of common sense; wisdom is the engagement of acquired sense.

7. Wisdom is the acquisition and intelligible application of the acquired knowledge.

8. Wisdom is thinking through the acquired knowledge to know what is required to make it work.

9. Wisdom is not a cheap commodity - it is a most costly treasure. (Job 28:12-18)

10. Wisdom is the costliest treasure of greatest value.

11. Wisdom carries a price.

12. Wisdom requires being studious.

13. Wisdom is, knowing the right steps to take from God and taking it.

14. Wisdom is, knowing the right place to go from God and going there.

15. Wisdom is, knowing the right thing to do from God and doing it.

16. The quality of your life and marriage is based on the quality of your references [Information, knowledge, insight and wisdom]. Every good marriage

is sustained by adequate relevant knowledge and continuous application of that acquired knowledge which is wisdom.

17. **Wisdom is not common sense - it is costly sense**: you read your way into greatness. **Wisdom must not be mistaken for common sense - it is the engagement of acquired sense**.

18. **Don't enter marriage with common sense**; rather do it with acquired sense and apply them to your marriage.

19. **Wisdom is not a cheap commodity - it demands your time, your energy and your resources.** Just as students don't fail exams because they don't know anything but because they don't know enough and because of wrong priorities, many also fail in their marriages because they don't know enough about marriage and have wrong priorities.

Abraham Lincoln said: 'I don't think much of a man who is not wiser today than he was yesterday.'

Henry Ford said: 'When you stop learning, you are old whether at 20 or 80 and when you keep learning you are young whether at 80 or at 20 – [therefore] the best thing to do is to keep your mind young through the art of learning or a commitment to life-long learning.'

20. Your sense of value for knowledge is a great

determinant of your great future in marriage.

21. **EVERY DAY OF YOUR LIFE AND MARRIAGE, YOU ARE EITHER BUILDING A LIBRARY OR A MORTUARY WITHOUT KNOWING!** Find what will take you there and stay with it. Someone asked my father in the Lord, "When do you make time to read?" He replied, 'When do you make time to eat?' And added: 'What eating is to you is what reading is to me.'

22. **Everything that works, works by knowledge.** You can't be a leader in anything if you are not willing to learn. It is your commitment to learning that brings out the best in you. You can't wish for a good marriage - you work at it.

23. **Wisdom guides you into continual satisfaction.** Isaiah 58:11, 'And the Lord shall guide thee continually, and satisfy thy soul in drought, and make fat thy bones: and thou shalt be like watered garden, and like a spring of water, whose waters fail not.'

24. **Wisdom says: THE GRASS IS NOT GREENER ELSEWHERE; IT IS GREENER WHERE YOU WATER IT!** The reason some people's garden looks nicer, greener and always blooming is continual heeding to guidance, instructions from the manual on maintaining a great garden.

25. **Watered gardens are not by accident.** They are deliberately planned for, cultivated, nurtured, charted and maintained.

26. **Every time someone looks at you, your marriage and family they are learning vital lessons to guide their lives by.** King Solomon said in Proverbs 24:30-34, 'I went by the field of the slothful, and by the vineyard of the man void of understanding; And, lo, it was all grown over with thorns, and nettles had covered the face thereof, and the stone wall thereof was broken down. Then I saw, and considered it well: I looked upon it, and received instruction. Yet a little sleep, a little slumber, a little folding of the hands to sleep: So shall thy poverty come as one that travelleth; and thy want as an armed man.'

27. **The difference between a watered garden, marriage, family, ministry and one overgrown with thorns and issues upon issues is adherence or non-adherence to instruction.** That's why the same Solomon said in Proverbs 4:13, 'Take fast hold of instruction; let [her] not go: keep her; for she [is] thy life.' and in Proverbs 19:20-21, 'Hear counsel, and receive instruction, that thou mayest be wise in thy latter end. There are] many devices in a man's heart; nevertheless the counsel of the Lord, that shall stand.'

28. **Getting married is easy. Staying married is hard work. Staying happily married is even harder work.** Prevention is the key so that you don't wake up one day asking yourself questions like: "Should I have married?" or "Should I stay married?" A few steps on your part toward improving your marriage will work wonders towards making your marriage strong, secure and content. Lack of skill, know-how is one of the reasons many don't stay married.

29. **FAMILIARIZE YOURSELF WITH THE KNOW-HOW OF MARRIAGE**: Ecclesiastes 10:10-17, 'If the iron be blunt, and he do not whet the edge, then must he put to more strength:' (If you are not using the right tools, principles, approach in your marriage, you will be using a lot of effort and energy and frustrate yourself and your whole house) but wisdom [is] profitable to direct. Surely the serpent will bite without enchantment; and a babbler is no better. The words of a wise man's [husband/wife's] mouth [are] gracious; but the lips of a fool will swallow up himself. The beginning of the words of his mouth [is] foolishness: and the end of his talk [is] mischievous madness. A fool also is full of words: a man cannot tell what shall be; and what shall be after him, who can tell him? the labour of the foolish (husband or wife) wearies [wears out] every one of them, because he **knoweth not how** (doesn't know how to marry

and stay married) to go to the city. (The marriage home) Woe to thee, O land, when thy king [is] a child, [husband or wife is a child or immature] and thy princes eat in the morning! (But) Blessed [art] thou, O land, when thy king [is] the son (mature through knowledge and wisdom [know-how]) of nobles, (acts maturely) thy princes eat in due season, for strength, and not for drunkenness!'

That is why you must search things out (Get my books: '200 questions you must ask before you say 'I DO'' and '101 Tips for a Great Marriage' from our website www.houseofjudah.org.uk) and make discoveries:

Proverbs 25:2, '[It is] the glory of God to conceal a thing: but the honour of kings [is] to search out a matter.'

You go on a search for the answers; they are there if you will care to look for them and not be lazy and end up with endless frustrations in your relationships.

30. Wisdom requires that you agree and settle among yourselves that divorce is not an option and will never even be mentioned. If you must stay in your marriage, you will be far likelier to work at the quality of it - i.e. your marriage. Do not use the word even as a threat or as a joke.

31. Wisdom demands that both of you need to have

a good communication link going on. If this doesn't happen, then disaster is just waiting to strike. If you have something on your mind, tell your spouse, just don't use "attack words" like "YOU ALWAYS", this is setting the conversation up for a frying pan swinging and sparks flying through the air.

32. **Marriage is not built on luck - it's built on choices. Fools believe in luck – the wise believe in the law of cause and effect.**

SECTION THREE:
COMMUNICATION: THE GREAT PRIORITY

12. Communicate with your spouse regularly. Regular dialogue, quick conversations during the day or debriefing at night will keep the lines of communication open.

Four Solid Foundation Stones for Good Communication

- Uphold The Priority Of Your Marriage
- Uphold The Permanence Of Your Marriage

- Uphold The Oneness Of Your Marriage
- Uphold The Openness Of Your Marriage

PRACTICAL INSIGHTS: The Components of Communication between Husband and wife

Each partner brings these areas into every communication:

- Your Consequential History
- Knowledge And Wisdom
- Past Experiences
- Self-Image
- Sense Of Humour
- **Current State**
- Emotions
- Mood
- **Current Conflicts**
- With others
- With each other
- With yourself

- With God
- At work
- **The Condition Of The Heart**
- Is it evil or good, heart of stone or flesh?
- **Matthew 12:35** 'A good man out of the good treasure of the heart bringeth forth good things: and an evil man out of the evil treasure bringeth forth evil things'
- **Ezekiel 36:26** 'A new heart also will I give you, and a new spirit will I put within you: and I will take away the stony heart out of your flesh, and I will give you an heart of flesh'
- **The Mouth:** The mouth speaks that which fills the heart-Mark 11:23
- **Matthew 12:34** 'O generation of vipers, how can ye, being evil, speak good things? For out of the abundance of the heart the mouth speaketh'
- **The Body**
- Body language
- Tone and volume of your voice

Sharpening Your Communication Skills

- Communication is to love what blood is to life
- Without communication love is dead
- Learn to communicate with your eyes
- Give the gift of your full attention
- Respond when he/she speaks to you
- Keep a confidence
- Avoid pat answers
- Allow your mate to open up about his or her fears
- Continually look for ways to build your mate's self-esteem
- When you talk, don't attack – talk to each other not at each other
- Never, never let the sun go down on your wrath
- The word "divorce" should never be in your vocabulary

How to Fight So Everybody Wins

Galatians 5:15, 'Watch out or you will be destroyed by each other'

Healthy relationships aren't conflict-free; they're conflict-resolving. The problem is: we fight for victories instead of fighting for solution. The result then is: one wins, one loses, and the relationship suffers! So, fight for solutions instead of personal victories.

Practical Insights for Fighting So That The Relationship Wins:

- Differences are inevitable, normal, and potentially beneficial.

- They're inevitable, because relationships bring together very different people.

- They're normal, because all relationships including great ones, experience them.

- They're potentially beneficial, because handled effectively, relationships grow through them.

Three Conflicting Handling Styles:

- The avoid style - these are the 'don't want to rock the boat' and 'let sleeping dogs lie' people

- The attack style - these are the 'get them before they get you' folk.

- The approach-assert style – these are the 'no price is too high for a good relationship' people

13. Don't shy away or keep silent about dealing with hard or controversial issues that must be addressed. Be genuine, respectful and courteous about your disagreement with your spouse. Engage in constructive criticism aimed at building and not tearing down. It will clear the air and help move communication to a deeper level. Keep it fair and be sure to reassure your spouse of your love and commitment as the motivation.

14. Keep complaints to yourself. Do not join in husband or wife-bashing when friends or family indulge. Show a healthy respect for your spouse by not airing your dirty laundry in public. Not only will your spouse feel bad if he/she should hear, but the friends you have complained to have long memories. Love does not keep a record of wrongs. (1 Corinthians 13) Discuss how you are feeling with your spouse.

15. Have separate interests and hobbies. Once in a while, communicate with your spouse the need to take time out by yourself in a retreat or a holiday [break]. By leaving the relationship for some time alone, you come back reenergized and renewed. You will have more to share if you have some time for yourself. Build Trust!

SECTION FOUR:

ROMANCE AND GENERAL MATTERS IN MARRIAGE

16. Go on dates, even after you have been married for years and especially if you have children. Carve out time for just you two, making dating a priority. Try new things together, take a class, find favourite places that you can revisit again and again and create memories together.

17. Work on you. There is very little you can do to change him or her. By working on your idiosyncrasies, bad habits and annoying traits, you have taken the first positive step. Marriage is not a contract but instead it is a covenant. You can't keep score and expect your marriage to flourish.

How to Make Your Wife Happy [things you need to know & do]:

You married the girl of your dreams, but how do you stay the man of hers? If you follow the right steps, you'll keep your wife happy for years to come.

18. First, you have to know what makes your wife happy. The things that you did to woo her aren't enough anymore. It's different when you're living marriage day to day. Like the saying goes: Ability can get you to the top but it takes character to keep you there! Does it make your wife happy when you vacuum, when you take out the trash, when you shower? Keep track of what it does for her.

19. DO WHAT MAKES HER HAPPY. If you know washing the dishes is high on her list, wash the dishes. Make habits of the things that make her happy. **Here's the big key:** Do what makes her happy without being asked. If you wash the dishes after she reminds you to wash the dishes, what good is that? Also, don't make a big deal of what you're doing. Don't say, "I'll wash the dishes tonight; you've had a hard day." Even though that's good, and she probably has had a hard day, it's better to do it as though it's something you wanted to do. Don't let her know you're doing it for points. Just do it. She'll notice.

20. Be sensitive to changes. Through the years, what makes your wife happy will change. Continue to be observant. Continue to anticipate. Continue to make her happy. **Marriage is made up of little things as much as it is made up of big ones.** Flowers, romantic dinners, spending quality time with her and jewellery all enhance relationship but so does balancing the cheque book, picking up after yourself.

21. Always put her first — before work, friends, even your favourite sport. **Act as if she's the best thing that ever happened to you, because we all know she is apart from Christ.**

22. Pick your fights/constructive discussions with care. Play fair. Show some class. Hurtful words can be forgiven, but they're hard to forget.

24. Fall in love again every day. Kiss her in taxis. Look across the room and wink at her. Tell her she's beautiful. Then tell her again.

25. Never miss an anniversary or a birthday or a chance to make a memory. Memories may not seem important now, but one day they'll be gold.

26. Always listen to her heart. If you're wrong, say you're sorry; if you're right, shut up.

27. Don't half-tie the knot; plan to stay married forever. No plan B.

28. Never go to bed mad; talk until you're over it, or you forget why you were mad. Ephesians 4:26, 'Be ye angry, and sin not: let not the sun go down upon your wrath.'

29. Laugh together a lot. If you can laugh at yourselves, you'll have plenty to laugh about. You live healthier and longer that way.

30. Remember that people are the least lovable when they are most in need of love [do things that don't warrant love.]

31. Never criticize, correct or interrupt her in public; try not to do it in private, either.

32. Never fall for the myth of perfectionism; it's a lie.

33. When you don't like each other, remember that you love each other; pray for and work at the "good days" to return and be sustained and they will. If life gives you a bitter experience don't get bitter, get better, just add lemon and sugar to your bitter experience and make a 'lemonade' out of it. There is always a way. (1 Corinthians 10:13)

34. Tell the truth, only the truth, with great kindness.

35. Kiss at least 10 seconds a day, all at once or spread out.

36. Memorize all her favourite things and amaze her with how very well you know her.

37. Examine your relationship as often as you change the oil in your car; keep steering it on a path you both want it to go.

38. Be content with what you have materially, honest

about where you are emotionally, and never stop growing spiritually.

39. Never raise your voice unless you're on fire (speaking in tongues – 'ragah') or the house is on fire.

40. Whisper when you argue.

41. Be both friends and lovers; in a blackout, light a candle, then make your own sparks.

42. Under no condition must you move your beddings downstairs or sleep alone on the couch. Even snoring can be discussed. There are ways.

43. Be determined to stay married. It is hard to stay married, if you are not already there.

44. Love your spouse. 'Yes, that sounds simple enough', you may say. But without love there isn't a marriage now, is there! Oh, remember: they have to love you too. You can't be in love with someone who doesn't love you. It works both ways – remember 100% not 50/50.

45. Be faithful and remain faithful. Your spouse would have to participate in this as well.

46. Stay sober. If one of you was addicted to drinking or drugging, give it up because it will not help your life long marriage plans. Don't be drunk with wine but the Spirit.

47. Try and get along with your spouses' friends. Not TOO chummy, but tolerate them. Drama should not be a major role in your relationship.

48. Surprise them sometime. Make breakfast in bed, take them out, bring home flowers, watch the kids and let them rest a while. Make a romantic bubble bath with candles for them.

49. Understanding. Try to understand their feelings. Try to avoid saying "I know exactly how you feel", because not one person can exactly understand another person's feelings. If there is something that bothers them, try and understand how you would feel if you were in that situation.

50. Public affection. Open doors [car, public, home], hold hands. Treat them like the King/Queen they are.

51. Be patient and honest with each other.

52. Be selfless.

53. Never give her a practical gift. If she really wants any kitchen utensil or bathroom product, let her go pick it out herself. There are certain things concerning the home which you must allow them to pick up themselves before you are sent back.

54. Lead your wife and family in all spiritual matters as the husband, go to church together, pray every day for each other and your marriage.

55. Cultivate family and friend relationships too. Keeping a strong group of genuine friends or maintaining 'genuine' family ties offers stability and allows your relationship to grow in context with other relationships.

56. Be an interesting person, lead your own life. But always save your best for each other. In the end, you will know you were better together than you ever could've been apart.

57. Finally, Never allow your love for each other to grow cold. Develop your love for each other to become as strong as death (Song of Solomon 8:6). Love is the major currency you trade and the greatest motivator in all you do.

SECTION FIVE:

MONEY MATTERS

IN MARRIAGE, YOU ARE EITHER BUILDING ON PRINCIPLES OR ON RUBBLES!

58. Learn and practice the healthy habit / art of 'delayed gratification'.

59. Don't let money get in the way of your undying ever-growing love for each other. Money is one of the leading causes of separation/divorce.

60. Put God first in all your monetary considerations. Pay your tithe consistently, joyfully, willingly, cheerfully, tirelessly and give generously in offerings to secure your marriage, family, destiny and future.

61. Plan for posterity, spiritually, physically, materially, mentally, financially and live a healthy life. Don't get your family into debt.

62. Keep no secrets. Pool your money together. Allow nothing and no one to come between you. Never hide your bank statements, bank account details, your salary or your monetary affairs from your spouse. If he or she is a spendthrift then mention it, discuss it, educate him/her and put things in place that the future is not squandered away through indiscipline, greed, selfishness or mismanagement. Spouses should compliment (and not conflict).

63. Never start your marriage insisting on maintaining your personal single accounts only. Operate a joint account and apply the 80/20% or 75/25% principle where the joint account is reserved for the majors and the 20/25% shared between both of you to be used for the minors - your personal needs/wants. Remember: Your money does not belong to you alone now but both of you within reason. [The two are one]

64. In the pursuit of your careers, professions, callings or ministry, **complete each other; don't compete with each other.** Never envy the progress, acceleration or success of your spouse especially your wife even if she earns more than you. Your attitude should be: Hey, it's our money.

65. Love her parents as your own, but don't ask them for money. Never criticize her family or friends. On her birthday, send flowers to her mother with a note saying, "Thank you for giving birth to the love of my life."

66. Never make your disagreements public. Marriage has winding roads (try not to make it public).

Remember, people are people (with strengths and weaknesses) including you. [Never use derogatory words against your spouse such as calling your wife or husband an idiot or a fool. No, you will be considered a bigger idiot or bigger fool to have chosen, dated, engaged, spent good money to marry an idiot and a fool, with your eyes wide open.]

67. Pay your bills on time and make sure you each have a living 'Will', a durable power of attorney and life insurance, lest, God forbid, you need them. Send a card for no reason. Surprise your spouse with a card, flowers or gift including money.

68. Spend money on your wife and vice versa.

69. Never allow money to be your master but your servant. When it comes to Money – Enjoy it now, use it as a servant, not your master and then pass it on. (Be addicted to giving, generosity and liberality)

70. ALWAYS REMEMBER THE TWO ARE NOW ONE – YOUR MONEY IS HER MONEY AND HER MONEY IS YOUR MONEY! HIS MONEY IS HER MONEY AND HER MONEY IS HIS MONEY BUT BE WISE IN HANDLING IT!

SECTION SIX:

SEXUAL MATTERS

71. Fulfil your scriptural obligations to your partner by knowing them as Adam knew his wife. Don't defraud each other and avoid timetables.

72. Prioritise your sex life.

- Don't leave it to chance or your spouse - plan for it.

- Be inventive.

- Be creative.

- Be innovative.

- Add spice and life.

- Invent new things to give it life and vibrancy always.

- Rub her feet and give her massages.

- Be sensitive, aware and responsive to each other's sexual needs and desires.

- Be open to new ideas and suggestions that will enhance your sex life including healthy books, CDs, DVDs, etc.

- It is very important that husbands and wives especially wives, learn to speak up regarding their sexual needs – these may sound like small things but they are the things that will keep the fire burning in a marriage. It's the little fixes that spoil the vine and the same other little additions that spark and adds to the enjoyment leading to satisfaction.

- Don't forget the little things – they matter and are the building blocks for the big things - Songs of Solomon 2:15.

- Ultimate success in everything depends to a great deal on giving attention to little things as much as the great things including romance and sex.

REMEMBER:

- Sex begins in the kitchen, I.e. Husband, don't sit there watching TV and changing channels all day expecting manifestations at night when you've left her to do all the house chores and she's worn out and say you will meet her upstairs. You'll wait till the second coming of Christ. Rather, if you don't want her to lie down like a timber [which you complain about] while you just come and take as may be your habit, then, assist her with the house chores so she's not worn out before you make love [have sex]. That way both of you are energized, actively involved, refreshed, satisfied and fulfilled.

- Sex is not a side issue with God – it is part of the marriage covenant.

- Sex is not love but an outward expression or demonstration of love.

- Sex is not spiritual. Sex is 100 percent physical and chemical.

- Sex is a spiritual union between two married people – a joining of spirit to spirit - a coupling of two people – a joining of flesh to flesh.

- Sex is an appetite God built into us when He created us; God designed us for appetites – you can call it cravings, drives, hungers, passions, whatever - it is still appetites.

- Sex is also for procreation – Genesis 1:28.

- Sex with our spouse is for recreation and release - it is for sheer joy and the pleasure it affords married couples.

- Sex is fun - God meant for us to enjoy sex; otherwise why would He have designed it to be so pleasurable?

- Sex is for communication – it is a loving environment that encourages communication, sexual consummation and provides an intimacy and communion that goes far beyond words.

- Sexual activity is restricted to marriage.

- Sexual relations are a normal part of a marriage - each spouse has the right to expect from the other as well as the responsibility to give to the other (1 Corinthians 7:3-5).

- Sexual fulfilment and happiness in marriage depends on an open, loving, accepting and affirming environment in which each spouse feels comfortable making his or her needs and desires known to each other.

- Concerning sexual behaviour: The question is not what we can get from each other but what we can give to each other and it is not about we can get away with, but what is healthy and edifying.

- Whatever we can do and be edified and not guilty afterwards is lawful and appropriate; if it does not edify, it is inappropriate.

- Discover from each other what satisfies each other i.e. your spouse and within healthy ethical boundaries and your faith, enjoy yourselves and satisfy each other.

- With sex, you must look good and fresh always.

- Look forward to making love to each other with eager, joyful, exciting anticipation. Be creative, innovative with the music, candles, the lights and in setting up the right atmosphere and conducive environment.

- Don't put a timetable or unreasonable restrictions on satisfying each other sexually.

- Remember the triangle and trapezium mentality and orientation of men and women so you don't leave the other dissatisfied - men are like triangles when it comes to sex - they look, admire, desire their woman and reach their climax and peak quicker but women require processing to reach a certain dimension before they can reach their peak/climax, hence what is called foreplay involving kissing, touching the sensitive parts for arousal before penetration. These are all pre-requisites that must be borne in mind and consciously worked at so no one is left dissatisfied.

- As much as possible both of you should discuss, study, work at and know what arouses you and deliberately and consciously work at doing it willingly and joyfully reaching your climax together or within close proximity of each other so both are satisfied and none is left wanting, feeling cheated or dissatisfied.

HEALTH BENEFITS OF SEX:

I came across this email: Please note that the contents of this email are not to be used to pressure your significant other in any way, "I'm Tired" means "I'm Tired"! Don't worry about the calories in those Valentine's Day chocolates – a proper celebration in the bedroom can help keep you in shape. In fact, sex can benefit your health in many ways. Here are seven reasons to give and get a little love – not just this special day, but any time.

1. Good for the heart: Sex is good for your heart. Like any physical exertion, sex is a form of cardio-exercise, which gets your heart pumping faster and helps it stay in shape. What's more, studies have shown that men who have sex two or more times per week cut their risk of a fatal heart attack by half.

2. Helps you lose weight: Like any form of exercise, sex helps you lose weight. Having sex for 30 minutes can burn off 85 calories. To put that in perspective: 15 minutes on the treadmill could burn up to 200 calories; 42 of these half-hour sessions, then, could shave a pound off your weight.

3. Boosts your immune system: While it's possible to contract a wide range of diseases, both from sex and from simple contact with others, safe sex between healthy partners can make you better equipped to fight illness. Those who have sex once or twice a week have been shown to have higher levels of immunoglobulin A or IgA, an antibody which helps protect you from respiratory diseases like the cold and flu.

Don't go overboard, though in studies, those who had sex three or more times a week had the lowest levels of antibodies.

4. Reduces the risk of prostate cancer: For younger men, sex reduces the risk of prostate cancer. Researchers have found that men in their 20s who had five or more ejaculations per week were one third less likely to develop the cancer in later life. Although they found no such correlation for older men, you could try to prove them wrong.

5. Relieves stress: There's a medical explanation for the mood boost sex gives you. The brain releases endorphins during and after sex, and these neurotransmitters create a feeling of euphoria while masking the negative effects of stress. Researchers have also found that sex lowers your blood pressure, which is good for your health and allows you to better keep your cool in stressful situations.

6. It relieves pain: Endorphins and lower blood pressure also mean that sex relieves pain. Endorphins are released during sex because of the heightened levels of the hormone oxytocin in your body. This has been known to alleviate arthritic and menstrual pain, among other things. Lower blood pressure can also help relieve migraines.

7. It helps you sleep: In addition to relieving stress and pain, the oxytocin generated during sex helps you sleep better. Sex relaxes you, promoting deeper, more restful sleep. What more do you need?

IN RELATION TO THIS SUBJECT AND PROBLEMS THAT SOME HAVE IN THEIR MARRIAGES, I WOULD LIKE TO SHARE WITH YOU THIS EMAIL THAT SOMEONE SENT ME ON SEX:

This is funny but sounds like the truth and it is written **"Ye shall know the truth and the truth will set you free"**

Sex from Pastor Khathide from Uganda's point of view:

A lot of people don't associate sex with God - they associate it with Satan and darkness, as if sex weren't holy. The Bible is explicit when it comes to sex. Sex is holy within marriage, and there is no prescribed style. Nowhere in the Bible does it say that the missionary position is the only sexual style. Not discussing sex in a relationship leads to divorce!!!! Pastor Khathide has counselled women who've complained: my husband treats me as if I were his brother. There was one who told him: I am tired of getting sex fortnightly, like a salary. Khathide told her she was lucky to be getting sex fortnightly, since some wives only get it on big days, like elections. Many husbands leave their wives to seek sexual pleasures in Hillbrow. Have you ever asked yourself what those wives have that you don't?

Wives have become very frigid and even sleep with their panties. If you're a married woman, you should sleep naked and let your bum touch your husband. Today you find men going out of their way to get a glimpse of a vagina [female sexual organ]. They page through magazines and even go to lingerie departments in stores hoping to see what's hidden under panties, **because their wives hide it from them.** Marriage is about being free with your body in front of your partner. A woman should parade naked and do some modelling to tempt her husband.

There are many married **women who don't know what their husbands' penises [male sexual organ] look like.** They only feel it when he enters her. They've never switched off the lights before undressing. **A penis is a wife's toy** - she is supposed to play with it. He blames couples for not making time for sex and complaining about being tired after a day's work. You find many couples who've been sexually starved for years.

God created sex for procreation and also for pleasure. You can't marry and not have a good time in bed. WHO SAID YOU CAN ONLY HAVE SEX AT NIGHT? Why can't you drive home during lunch and have a quickie with your wife? We're all equal in sex - it's not just about a woman satisfying a man.

You have to satisfy each other. Have you ever seen a woman who has been satisfied? Have you noticed how she glows and becomes energetic? May the Lord Bless you! This is the "Whole Truth, and Nothing But the Truth." So God Help Us From The Beginning.

SECTION SEVEN:

GRATITUDE, THANKFULNESS, PRAISE AND JOYFULNESS

73. NEVER MURMUR, GRUMBLE, COMPLAIN, WHINE OR BE DISSATISFIED – ALWAYS BE GRATEFUL!

REMEMBER: Thankful people always have their tanks full!

a. In the world, you give thanks after you receive something but in the kingdom you give thanks before you receive something or see anything. Philippians 4:6-8, "Be careful for nothing; but in every thing by prayer and supplication with thanksgiving let your requests be made known unto God. And the peace of God, which passeth all understanding, shall keep your hearts and minds through Christ Jesus."

b. Gratitude is a covenant attitude and so is thankfulness. Just as the reason for many people's frustrated lives and endless frustration in marriage is ingratitude, thanklessness and joylessness, in the same way, the sole reason for many people's fulfilled lives and ever-blossoming marriages is gratitude, thankfulness and joyfulness.

c. God cannot stand or remain in a joyless environment: (Psalm 22:3) 'But thou art holy, O thou that inhabitest the praises of Israel.'

d. Many people's dry and fruitless marriages is traceable to their joyless countenance as revealed in Joel 1:12 says, 'The vine is dried up, and the fig tree languisheth; the pomegranate tree, the palm tree also, and the apple tree, even all the trees of the field, are withered: because JOY IS WITHERED AWAY FROM THE SONS OF MEN.'

So, your joyless attitude, countenance and environment could be the reason for your dry life and dryness in your marriage relationship. Sarah and her husband Abraham despite their circumstances believed God's word and aligned their countenance by faith to conform to and demonstrate the meaning of their new names (Sarah meaning mother of many nations and Abraham meaning father of many nations) at a time when both of them were past MENOPAUSE AND PAPAPAUSE = MEGAPAUSE) and put up the acceptable behaviour by calling the things that be not or was not as though they were) which culminated in them physically seeing and embracing the child they confessed i.e. Isaac nine months later. So did Hannah in 1 Samuel 1 and the Shunemite woman in 2 Kings 4.

e. JOY IS A CHOICE: Joy is a choice you make in the face of bad news, challenges, problems, calamity, trouble, lack, shortage, insufficiency, a down economy childlessness or disagreement with your spouse. With all these in mind, Jesus said in John 16:33, 'These things I have spoken unto you, that in me ye might have peace. In the world ye shall have tribulation: BUT BE OF GOOD CHEER I HAVE OVERCOME THE WORLD.' (It's a choice, a decision you make to be of good cheer; irrespective.)

f. REMEMBER: **IT'S NOT BECAUSE THINGS ARE BAD THAT YOU ARE SAD; IT'S BECAUSE YOU ARE SAD THAT'S WHY THINGS ARE BAD**:

- Proverbs 17:22, 'A merry heart doeth good like a medicine: but a broken spirit drieth the bones.'

I repeat: **It's not because things are bad that you are sad; it's because you are sad that's why things are bad in your marriage**, so stay joyful, grateful, thankful and praiseful irrespective. Because Joy is withered away from married couples that is why the vine [their marriage] is dried up, and the fig tree [romantic life] languisheth; the pomegranate tree, [social life] the palm tree also, and the apple tree, [communication] even all the trees of the field, [sex life] are withered:

g. SO, MAINTAIN YOUR JOY! **YOU ARE NOT BREAKING DOWN BECAUSE YOU ARE SUFFERING BREAK DOWN, NO! YOU ARE SUFFERING BREAKDOWN BECAUSE YOU ARE BREAKING DOWN**: You are suffering break down in your body and marriage because you are breaking down in your mind, which is now affecting your body and every area of your family life.

I PROPHESY TO YOU THAT FROM TODAY,

JOY TAKES OVER AND YOUR MARRIAGE EXPERIENCES TOTAL RECOVERY IN JESUS' NAME! (Joel 2:25-27, 'And I will restore to you the years that the locust hath eaten, the cankerworm, and the caterpillar, and the palmerworm, my great army which I sent among you. And ye shall eat in plenty, and be satisfied, and praise the name of the LORD your God, that hath dealt wondrously with you: and my people shall never be ashamed. And ye shall know that I am in the midst of Israel, and that I am the LORD your God, and none else: and my people shall never be ashamed.'

74. STAY THANKFUL, PRAISEFUL AND FULL OF GRATITUDE TO GOD FOR THIS PRIVILEGE!

75. Welcome each other home with expectation, eagerness, excitement and occasional surprises. End each day with prayer, thanksgiving, praise to God and a hug, a peck, a kiss or a cuddle for your spouse - if it leads to the bonus of you 'knowing each other scripturally' like Adam did with Eve, PRAISE GOD and if not, still PRAISE GOD!

PART TWO

What Men [Husbands] Want From Their Women [Wives] & What Women [Wives] 'Really' Want From Their Men [Husbands]

I read somewhere that: 'Today's women have achieved more than their great grandmothers could have ever imagined. Women are in politics, women are in space; women are excelling in every career imaginable. Women today are strong, independent and sexually liberated. Despite the females' social evolution, however, you may be surprised to learn that women actually still enjoy being treated like women, and they still appreciate a little **courtesy** now and then. The two sexes seem to be so different but really are quite alike, men always wonder what exactly is going through a woman's mind. Men seldom seem to understand a woman's thought process. The same is true for her; she always wonders, what do men really want from women.

To understand your man you should recognize that both men and women are actually looking for the same things, though they state it quite differently.'

I have pulled my hair out a couple of times over the

past 24 years until I begun to learn about this subject from credible sources with proofs. Like I said in my previous book, 200 questions you must ask, investigate and know before you say, 'I DO' I came into this raw knowing nothing and made several mistakes. Thank God no one calls me mad now! **I know better!**

The following are some initial thoughts for what men and women initially look for and continue to expect from each other in marriage: As usual the women's outweigh the men [245 to 115] leaving us with more to do! WE WON'T HAVE IT ANY OTHER WAY!

Chapter Three

WHAT WOMEN 'REALLY' WANT

[What your Wife really wants]

Your Wife's Needs:
245 'COMMANDMENTS'/SUGGESTIONS

245 practical ways to make your wife happy, content and satisfied with you, responsive to you, secure and fulfilled in her marriage.

When a woman's needs are met, she gains security and glows with a sense of well-being. Some of her glow will rub off on you, especially if you are responsible for it in the first place. To satisfy your wife, you need to make a deliberate effort to meet each of her needs listed, explained and amplified below:

As a Husband: (Ephesians 5:25-33; 1 Peter 3:7)

1. You must love and care for your wife. (Ephesians

5:23)

2. If you know how to treat your woman, she'll build you up wherever you are; her heart will be with you to lift you up to the heights. (Proverbs 31) If not she'll pull you down quick. Women can either make you or break you.

3. The bodies of women are built for affection, love and comfort, so, show it.

4. The bodies of men are built to provide strength, warmth (feet-warming of your wife's cold feet in bed) and security so provide all.

5. Show your wife affection, love, shower her with praises, appreciate her and make boast of her generally and in the Lord – her cooking, her looks, etc.

6. Do whatever it takes to let her heart be with you always. When you go out in the field, your wife's heart must be out there with you.

7. When there is a choice between wealth, riches, property and the husband's affection and love, a real woman will choose the latter except some weird women who will not even let you give a penny to those in need.

8. The only language a woman understands is love and affection. That is why you see very pretty women going out with a not so gorgeous or handsome man. Why? Because the man has been able to sweep her off her feet with a great show of affection; that is – love, affection and attention is at work. Don't get tired of showing it.

9. Set aside quality time for your wife – put the children to bed together or divide the work among you and take a break together, sometimes. Date her every week or every two weeks and have a honey moon every six months.

10. Husbands are supposed to grow up and act maturely - reason being any husband who continually behaves as a child, indirectly turns his wife into his mother and this can have a serious and devastating effect on their love life i.e. romantic and sexual lives because no man can make love to his mother. So husbands keep your wives as wives - don't force them to become your mother by your constant childish behaviours.

11. A woman needs to be in harmony with her husband through a deep intimate relationship.

She needs comradeship, harmony and a feeling of togetherness and acceptance.

12. Love her unconditionally.

13. Your wife needs to feel that she is very valuable in your life, more important than your mother, father, children, friends, your secretary and your job.

14. She needs to know that you are willing to share an intimate moment of comfort with her without demanding explanation or giving lectures.

15. She needs open, attentive and uninterrupted communication.

16. She needs to be praised so she can feel a valuable part of your life.

17. She needs to feel free to help you without fearing retaliation, insecurity or anger.

18. She needs to know that you will defend and protect her always.

19. She needs to know her opinion is so valuable that you will discuss issues with her before making joint decisions and that you will act only after carefully and thoroughly evaluating her advice.

20. She needs to share her life with you in every area, i.e. the home, family and outside interests.

21. She needs you to be the kind of man her son can and would like to follow and her daughter would want to marry.

22. Communicate with her; never close her out, disregard or ignore her.

23. Regard her as important, very essential and an invaluable asset.

24. Do everything you can to understand her feelings; there are times when you don't have to try to solve her problems, just let her know you understand; that's all she wants to hear from you. A wife narrates an issue to her husband, and the husband [man-side of him, being a solver of problems] just wants to solve her problem but all she wants you to say is 'I understand how you feel, It will be alright and we will deal with it together.' That is, later on when she is ready for the solution, not before.

25. Be interested in her friends who have her welfare at heart.

26. Ask her opinion frequently.

27. Value what she says.

28. Let her feel your approval and affection always.

29. Protect her on a daily basis.

30. Be gentle and tender with her.

31. Develop and maintain a sense of humour.

32. Avoid sudden major changes without discussion and giving her time to adjust.

33. Learn to respond openly and verbally when she wants to communicate with you.

34. Comfort her when she is down emotionally. For instance, put your arms around her and silently, hold her for a few seconds without lectures or put-downs.

35. Be interested in what she feels is important in life even though you may not think it is.

36. Correct her gently and tenderly.

37. Allow her to teach you what she is good at without putting up your male 'macho' defenses.

38. Make quality, special, uninterrupted time available for her and your children at least once a week.

39. Be trustworthy, i.e. be someone she can trust.

40. Compliment her often.

41. Be creative when you express your love, either in words or actions.

42. Have specific family goals for each year.

43. Allow her to buy things she considers necessary.

44. Be forgiving when she offends you without bringing it up again.

45. Show her you need her.

46. Accept her the way she is; discover her uniqueness and acknowledge that it is special.

47. Admit your mistakes and remain humble.

48. Lead your family in their spiritual relationship with the Lord.

49. Let her lean on you as the man that can be relied on, counted on and depended on and not you lean on her with complaints and acts, tantrums and behaviors of insecurity.

50. Be decisive.

51. Be the man at home.

52. Be the ever-present husband.

53. Be the ever-present Father at home, not an absentee father.

54. Be the Priest in the home, lead, live and show the way.

55. Be the king at home and she will be a queen to you at home.

56. Allow your wife to attempt and fail sometimes; then discuss what went wrong or could have been done or approached in a better way after you have comforted her.

57. Rub her feet or neck after a hard day at work and volunteer to cook the dinner and wash the dishes after you've run her a bath.

58. Bring her breakfast in bed occasionally.

59. Take time for just the two of you to sit down and talk calmly.

60. Go on walks and romantic outings together.

61. Write her a letter occasionally, telling her how much you love her and buy her cards that

express your undying and ever-increasing love and appreciation for her.

62. Surprise her with a card, flowers or gift.

63. Express how much you appreciate her in word and deeds.

64. Tell her how proud you are of her.

65. Defend her to others both in her presence and in her absence.

66. Prefer her over others.

67. Give advice in a loving way when she asks for it.

68. Do not expect her to do activities beyond her emotional or physical capabilities.

69. Pray for her to enjoy God's best in life.

70. Take time to notice, acknowledge and appreciate her for what she has done for you and the family.

71. Brag about her to other people behind her back, i.e. in her absence.

72. Share your thoughts and feelings with her.

73. Tell her about your job if she is interested.

74. Take time to see how she spends her day, at work or at home.

75. Learn to enjoy what she enjoys.

76. Take care of the kids [younger children] before dinner.

77. Help straighten up the house before dinner.

78. Occasionally let her take a bubble bath while you do the dishes.

79. Understand her physical limitations and help out if you have several children.

80. Discipline the children in love, not anger.

81. Help her attain her goals - such as education, career, hobbies, destiny, etc.

82. Treat her as if God stamped on her forehead, "Handle with care."

83. Get rid of habits that annoy her or get her upset.

84. Be gentle and thoughtful to her relatives.

85. Do not compare her relatives with yours in a

negative way.

86. Thank her for things she has done without expecting anything in return.

87. Do not expect a band to play whenever you help with the housecleaning.

88. Make sure she understands everything you are planning to do.

89. Do little things for her – an unexpected kiss, coffee or cold drink in bed.

90. Treat her as an intellectual equal.

91. Find out if she wants to be treated as physically weaker (1 Peter 3:7).

92. Discover her fears in life and encourage and protect her.

93. See what you can do to eliminate her fears.

94. Discover her sexual needs.

95. Ask if she wants to discuss how you can meet her sexual needs.

96. Find out what makes her insecure.

97. Plan your future together.

98. **Do not quarrel over words**, but **try to find the hidden meanings behind the words spoken**, i.e. **find out what she meant, not what she said!**

99. Practice common courtesies like holding the door for her, pouring her coffee.

100. Ask if you offend her sexually in any way.

101. Ask if she is jealous or suspicious of anyone or insecure in any way.

102. See if she is uncomfortable about the way money is spent.

103. Take her on dates now and then.

104. Hold her hand in public.

105. Put your arm around her in front of friends.

106. Tell her you love her – often, in word and deeds.

107. Remember anniversaries, birthdays, and other special occasions. (If you want to live long.)

108. Learn to enjoy shopping with her. [that's a tough one – I must admit]

109. Teach her to hunt and fish or whatever you

enjoy doing.

110. Give her a special gift from time to time.

111. Share the responsibilities around the house.

112. Do not belittle her feminine characteristics.

113. Let her express herself freely, without fear of being called stupid or illogical.

114. Choose your words carefully, especially when angry. (Some women are elephants!)

115. Do not criticize her in front of others.

116. Do not let her see you become excited about the physical beauty or features of another woman – it is improper and disrespectful.

117. Be sensitive to other people.

118. Let your family know you want to spend special time with them.

119. Fix dinner for her from time to time.

120. Be sympathetic when she is sick.

121. Call her when you are going to be late.

122. Do not disagree with her in front of the children.

123. Take her out to dinner/lunch and for weekend 'get–aways'.

124. Do the "little things" she needs from time to time.

125. Give her special time to be alone or with her [good/well-meaning] friends.

126. Buy her what she considers an intimate gift.

127. Read a book she recommends to you.

128. Give her an engraved plaque assuring her of your lasting love.

129. Write her a poem about how special she is.

130. Look into her eyes lovingly.

131. Look at her longingly.

132. Genuinely admire her looks and her figure.

133. Assure her that you love her.

134. Show continued and uninterrupted love for her so that she can feel that she comes first in your life.

135. Comment favourably on her attractiveness, especially when she is smartly dressed - "you look

charming in this dress; you look sensational.'

136. Show appreciation for the way she performs her numerous roles in the home.

137. Demonstrate your love by an occasional embrace or caress.

138. Remember her birthday, and give her presents on such occasions.

139. Give her occasional gifts, especially when you have been away for a while. It assures her that you have her at heart. Note: these gifts do not have to be expensive.

140. Accept her as an equal partner at home and consult her when making decisions about the home, the children's education and upbringing, and about other members of the family. Even if her advice is not taken, her views should be respected.

141. Before you buy something for the home, it is better to discuss it with your wife first. This is because, most women are particular about the decorations in the hall and sitting room, the type and colour of the bed sheets, the curtains, and other decorative materials, such as things needed for the kitchen, the toilets and so on.

You will do well to give her a free hand to do this, and to show confidence in her ability as the builder of the home.

142. Share with her your social, spiritual, and other activities. Don't leave her alone at home. Occasionally, take her out on outings.

143. Have a good wash before going to bed.

144. Go to church with her and be actively involved in a department in the church. A woman wants to share every aspect of her husband's life with him.

145. Always dress up and appear simple, smart, neat, clean-shaven, trimmed hair, moustache and beard using a good cologne to ensure that you smell good always and look sharp. Wives pride themselves in their man's looks and being able to proudly point a finger at him and say, "That is my husband".

146. Be and remain faithful to your wife and your wife only and drink water out of her cisterns only 'sexually'. Flirting with another woman degrades your wife, makes her feel she is second best, and tarnishes your reputation. It can also result in unexpected pregnancies

and the birth of unplanned for and unwanted children. Someone also said, 'Girl friends are more expensive than wives.' A third party will result in your financial resources being stretched further than it should and additional avoidable expenses and responsibilities.

147. Take up and fulfil your God-given professional role as head of the home. Every woman wants her husband to be "the man in the home, the one who maintains home discipline, initiates action for the welfare of the family, and plays such roles as will make her feel that he is the leader." Failure to do this effectively and consistently in the home results in the wife being tempted to take up the leadership role culminating in reversal of roles and chaos. Remember, 'Women become men when men stop being men.'

148. Create an atmosphere for sharing in the home by making it possible for easy communication to take place with your wife in the home as a sign that you accept her as part of yourself. For example crack jokes, play games together, or talk about current affairs-the political, economic, and social conditions of the day: that will make all the difference to the marriage.

149. Comment more on the good parts of your wife and less on her failures!

150. Eat and genuinely enjoy your wife's food and prefer it above any other person's food on this planet and boldly acknowledge and declare it both privately and publicly. Don't you ever reject or abandon your wife's food to go and eat somewhere else because of a misunderstanding. It is childish, highly irregular, totally unacceptable conduct and behaviour which also raises serious questions and suspicions of unfaithfulness and extra marital affairs.

151. Your salary and/or wages [both salaries and/or wages] must be known and open without reservation to both of you. Open knowledge of this eradicates suspicion and will enable you to plan accurately for your present and your future. Proper planning for the future welfare of the family depends on the ability of the couple to pool their financial resources together. There are many ways of doing this but the essential thing is for the couple to regard what each brings home as "ours", and not "his" or "hers".

152. This will also make for effective planning for housing, education of children, and for security

against old age and death of either partner. This is one area where a husband should take the initiative to draw the wife to himself.

153. As head of the home a man must do whatever he can do to make his wife's work at home lighter for her. We live in an era when as a result of socio-economic pressures many women have to take up full-time employment outside the home in addition to their household duties. Thus both the man and his wife return home after work already tired. This is why the husband should share in the household activities. He can bathe and feed the children whilst the wife is busy in the kitchen, and help clear the table after meals as the wife undertakes the washing of the plates. He can also help to make the bed. A husband who helps in household activities does not only help to relieve the wife of too much burden, he also saves time for the couple to relax in each other's company.

154. Don't starve your wife sexually; your body is hers and hers is yours. Do not defraud each other. (1 Corinthians 7:5)

155. Make your wife feel good about herself.

156. Value the same things in your wife that you

value in yourself.

157. Make sure your face spontaneously breaks into a smile when you see your wife.

158. When you leave the house, let your wife have a sense of well-being having been nourished by your company.

159. Tell each other honestly what you really want instead of using manipulation or games.

160. Don't think less of your wife when she gets angry with you.

161. Accept your wife as she is instead of having several plans to redo her.

162. Let your behavior be consistent with your words.

163. Let your actions show you really care for your wife.

164. Enjoy introducing your wife to your friends or acquaintances.

165. Be sincere enough to share with your wife your moments of weakness, failure and disappointment. She is your friend.

166. Let your wife say of you that you are a good listener.

167. Trust your wife to solve her own problems sometimes.

168. Admit to your wife you have problems or challenges and need her comfort and encouragement sometimes.

169. Create interest in her when you share things you consider important.

170. Learn from your wife and value what she says.

171. Let your wife feel she's more important to you than anyone or anything else in your life, except for your relationship with Christ Jesus.

172. Let your wife know and be fully persuaded that if anything ever happened to you she will be the first person you would call and not your best friend.

173. Endeavour to know at least five of your wife's major needs and how to meet those needs in a skillful way.

174. Make sure you know what your wife needs when she's under stress or when she's discouraged.

175. When you offend your wife make sure you usually admit you were wrong and seek her forgiveness.

176. Praise your wife at least once a day.

177. Let your wife say of you, you are open to her correction.

178. Let your wife describe you as a protector and that you know what her limitations are as a woman.

179. Let your wife say of you that you usually consider her feelings and ideas whenever making a major decision that affects the family or her.

180. Assure your wife that you enjoy being with her and sharing many of life's experiences with her.

181. Let your wife say of you, you are a good example of what you would like her to be.

182. Don't underestimate your wife.

183. Encourage your wife to discover, develop and release her full potential as a woman.

184. Help bring out the best in your wife; encourage her to aim high.

185. Encourage and empower your wife to fulfill her destiny.

186. Respect your wife's intuitive abilities – it will save you a whole lot.

187. Listen to your wife – don't only hear – listen!

188. Give her a cuddle sometimes without having any funny ideas.

189. When you are not sure of what you do sometimes, let her lead the way in the bedroom.

190. If your wife persistently reacts negatively to you, it may be because she perceives a threat to one or both of two important areas:

    (1) Her security

    (2) Her established relationships.

    Very often what women want is not what most men expect! The following are an additional list of what I discovered from other resource materials of what women/wives want from their men/husbands: JUST WHEN YOU THOUGHT YOU HAD DONE MORE THAN ENOUGH HUH!

191. What a woman really wants from you as a man is that you display confidence and masculinity

and allow her to feel safe around you; i.e. safe to be a woman and be 'girly', safe that you will be confident enough to make the right decisions about anything and everything at the right times.

192. Women also want a man that has the courage to walk over and actually start a conversation both before and within marriage. The fire shouldn't burn out. Be an initiator too!

They want a man/husband who will:

193. Be head of the home. (1 Corinthians 11:13)

194. Provide for the family. (1 Timothy 5:8)

195. Train the children. (1 Timothy 3:4-5)

196. Be Faithful to one wife. (1 Timothy 3:12)

197. Love them as their wife unconditionally. (Ephesians 5:25)

198. Be attentive to them.

199. Be a good listener.

200. Be caring.

201. Be gentle.

202. Interact with them in a way that:

- Makes her feel appreciated, very special and

wanted.

- Makes them feel sexual attraction for you.

- Is fun and interesting.

- Includes flirting and humour.

A man/husband who:

203. **Makes her feel special: Some women have said:** 'Buy me flowers and I'll ask for a vase. Buy me chocolates and I'll gain two pounds. But write me a letter telling me how you feel about me? I would probably frame it.' Making your woman feel special takes effort, but it goes much further than a corny, meaningless, hallmark-packaged "gesture" would. It means a great deal!

204. **Challenges her positively:** Appeal to the great potential in her and motivate her to be all she can be. Don't be afraid to tell her she is wrong and don't give her whatever she wants. That's the husband she wants.

205. **Knows how to 'man up':** The term is confusing, because women still want men who share their emotions and groom themselves properly. But women don't think it's manly to act overly macho anymore; they would prefer you have meaningful

goals, pursue them and learn responsibility and behave responsibly. Some say: I could care less if you choose a career or a family to man up – the important thing is you actually choose to do so!

206. **Is not boring but visionary, engaging and creative in conversation and taking initiatives:** A husband going somewhere in particular in life.

207. **Dates her before the marriage and consciously plans for more dates, outings, holidays and surprising her with things she likes during their marriage:** A man who doesn't do all the dating before marriage but reserves some [the best] for the marriage – more!

208. **Returns her calls/texts/messages**: Many women gage a man's interest level by how long it takes him to respond when she contacts him. If his response time is poor, she might assume he's just not that into her both before and within marriage. Now, it's no secret that women and men have differing opinions on what constitutes good communication, and we're not saying you need to drop everything the minute she calls. She knows you're a busy man; she's busy too. What women want from men is a call back as soon as they're able, as opposed to sometime

the following day. This doesn't mean you have to send an e-mail or a text of epic proportions if you don't have time; a sentence or two will suffice to make her feel like you care which is all she really wants to know.

209. **Kisses her for no reason:** As much as they love sex, women also enjoy a nice, deep kiss that doesn't have any strings attached. This serves two purposes: It lets her indulge in kissing for the sheer pleasure of it, and it also tells her you want her, and not just sex. Yes, you're charming and sexy and she loves being naughty for you, but sometimes she needs a different type of connection. To really do what women want from men, try a surprise kiss for no reason at all; she'll love you for it. Combine this with a little hand-holding and she'll be smiling for days.

210. **Touches her often: it sends the signal of assurance -** 'I care, I love you and I am here.'

211. **Dances with her:** Simply put, dancing with a woman makes her feel special. Unfortunately, most men are reluctant to put their dancing shoes on, especially in a public setting. Guess what? While she'd probably welcome the idea, you don't need to visit a nightclub to dance with your woman. She'll be just as thrilled if

you slipped your favourite song in the CD player and danced with her in the living room. This would actually be to your advantage, as you have total control over the music. You're also conveniently located if the dancing starts to lead to the throne…..

212. **Dresses up for her:** Dressing up to take your woman out is an excellent way to impress her. It's not about the clothes; it's about the fact that you find her worth dressing up for. It lets her know that you think she's worth that kind of effort. Besides, a nice shirt and dress pants can increase your sex appeal by leaps and bounds; you may feel overdressed, but your hotness factor will have magnified exponentially. It's true what they say: Women really do love a sharp-dressed man.

213. **Lies closer, cuddles her and warms her up in bed especially her cold feet:** Your body is build to provide warmth to your woman. You may not feel like warming her feet because you need warming yourself – just do it! Score points carry forward!

214. **Remembers random milestones:** As a rule, birthdays, date and place you met or proposed [if you can remember], valentine's day,

memorable moments and anniversaries should always be remembered; forgetting something of this magnitude will send the message that you don't find her terribly important. After all, she probably memorized yours earlier on in the relationship, so if hers goes unnoticed, she'll be utterly heartbroken. Here's how to do what women want from men: To truly impress her, aim to remember the insignificant dates, as well as the big ones. The first time you told her you loved her, the first time you kissed, the first place you vacationed together, what she was wearing the first time you met. Any one of these will turn her to jelly and score you more bonus points than you can shake a stick at.

215. **Buys her what she likes knowingly or surprises her:** In consultation with her and sometimes unknowingly, buy her the clothes you like to see her wear at home and for outings.

216. **Sets aside quality time to spend with her and be there:** Don't prioritize or allow anything or anyone to come between you [your friendship].

217. **Takes on an activity with her:** What women want from men is to spend time with their man outside of the bedroom. They want to

experience life with their man, and this is one of the best ways to develop a three-dimensional relationship. If neither of you are the sporty type, try something else that you already excel at. Teach her how to play table tennis or what you love doing gradually if she's interested - she'll love the personalized attention.

218. **Proposes a visit to her family or buys her a ticket to go on holidays by herself to rest:** Women love it when a man gets along with her genuine, well-meaning friends, but she simply adores it when he gets along with her family. Even if you're not particularly fond of her busybody mother and father, suggesting a visit (even just a yearly one) can really make your woman's day. It lets her know you recognize the importance of family. This is truly the kind of suggestion that leads to a warm and fuzzy feeling, so don't be afraid to suggest it. Book a ticket for her to go see them and spend some time with them; it means a whole lot to them.

219. **Pays attention to the little things. It's always the little things:** When it comes to what women want from men, the little things really do matter. The items on this list aren't particularly difficult or time-consuming, but they are, unfortunately, very often overlooked by men. This often leads

a woman to feel neglected, which in turn leads to nagging and other problems. Make her feel special, and she'll go to the ends of the earth for you; try one of these suggestions listed above and she'll feel like you've already gone there and back for her.

220. **Is confident:** Women just love truly confident men. Men who know what they are about, are visionary, passionate about what they believe, their purpose in life, what they want from life, how to get it and who are so determined they go all out to get it; Men who don't give up easily, don't take 'no' for an answer, are persistent, don't tolerate and hate with a passion the statement 'It can't be done'. Confidence is an attitude thing. In particular, male confidence frequently manifests as an "I-can-handle-it attitude". This does not mean that feelings are denied. It doesn't imply an absence of doubt, fear, or vulnerability but is met with courage which is not the absence of fear but a mastery of it Confidence simply says: "I can deal with it… somehow… well at least I'll give it my best shot". The attitude of confidence doesn't even have to be constant, just generally present in the face of most of life's challenges. Women

instinctually look for clues to a man's level of confidence... and test it to the limit...

The good news is: Confidence is primarily an attitude toward meeting the challenges of life before they become problems of which we all know there's no shortage of. Willingness to face seeming insurmountable challenges is still the ultimate key to a woman's respect. It is not the specific activity that a man engages in that matters, what matters is what goes on in the man's head that makes him feel some sense of Mastery. Although a woman likes to believe a man is willing to deal with a lot of things, what really counts is that he is able to deal with her.

Wives are looking for a Man/Husband who give her:

221. Undivided Attention.

222. Affirmations.

223. Demonstrative love.

224. Pays her Compliments.

225. Genuine Affection.

226. Gives both of them Interesting lives.

227. Warmth toward her and their children.

228. Adequate financial resources.

229. Who is Polite and respectful.

230. Emotional openness.

231. Relationship with Long-term potential.

232. Good surprises.

233. Men who take initiatives in the interest of their partners.

234. A generous man and consistent provider.

235. A fabulous father to their children.

236. A selfless man.

237. Smart dresser

238. Sharp looking

239. A man who makes her feel more special than everyone else – privately and publicly.

240. One who brings a smile to her face whenever they meet privately and publicly [or most times].

241. A man who boosts her morale

242. Who will, nurture, harness, cultivate and release

the jewels [potential] in her.

243. Patient enough to train by example and teach her what he knows without making her feel useless or stupid.

244. A man they can boast of and call 'my man'.

245. Treats her like the queen that she is, has always been and will continue to be in his eyes.

What women don't want:
- Inept come-on lines [fake raps]
- Sloppy looks
- Self centeredness
- Arrogance
- Slimy, over eagerness
- Roughness
- A 'weakling' who faints at the slightest sign of challenges
- Competition
- Dishonesty
- Infidelity
- An Aimless man
- A Lazy man
- An abuser
- Molester
- Indecisiveness
- Unfaithfulness

- A non-provider
- Hurtful words that cut deep
- Flattery
- Making them look stupid
- Annoying habits
- Sex without adequate preparation
- Always consulting with parents before making crucial decisions
- Makes decisions unilaterally without her involvement

[FOR MORE INSIGHT, GET MY BOOKS: 101 TIPS FOR A GREAT MARRIAGE; 200 QUESTIONS YOU MUST ASK, INVESTIGATE AND KNOW BEFORE YOU SAY 'I DO' from our website: www.houseofjudah.org.uk]

Chapter Four

WHAT MEN WANT

[What your Husband wants]

WHAT EVERY HUSBAND NEEDS TO MAKE HIM LIVE HAPPILY EVER AFTER WITH HIS WIFE

As a Wife: (Ephesians 5:25-33; 1 Peter 3:7)

Recently, an online survey discovered that apart from a woman being spiritual [biblically] with non-negotiable virtues, also in the natural, i.e. on the physical level, men preferred women with an average size body and curves to those whose bodies bared more bone than fat; like the models we see on the runways. However, even while an average size body did get the attention of the men it was actually a woman's personality that men considered beautiful the most. They also thought that a woman with self-confidence is beautiful. Being kind, caring and sincere were three other attributes that were also considered beautiful in a woman as well as a woman who was always cheerful with a beautiful attractive smile and countenance willing to listen to him and engage in honest, decent, sincere, sensible and productive conversation with him.

As far as looks were concerned, i.e. physical attributes, 'the eyes have it'. Men also confessed that women with natural average-sized breasts were more beautiful than women with breast implants and when it came to women's fashion they thought women looked beautiful in casual clothing verses neat. And what underwear did they find beautiful on a woman? Surprisingly, average and feminine beat out the skimpy erotic panties found on models in adult magazines. Even more surprising, the surveys found that men thought women with a barely there, natural makeup looked more beautiful than women who wear a lot of makeup.

Apparently average men are finding out that there's more than meets the eye when it comes to a woman being beautiful. Men would rather get to know a woman and discover that she is beautiful naturally instead of just judging her from the way she looks and finding out that she's really an ugly person on the inside. They're discovering what we've known all along, that true beauty lies within. The virtues listed in Proverbs 31 still have their place in priorities and qualities most men look for when deciding who to choose/marry and remain with or stay married to as partners for life.

115 EXPECTATIONS OF YOUR HUSBAND:

1. Be a loving wife.

2. Maintain your gorgeous looks and sexual attraction because it is one of the basic reasons why people marry.

3. Make every effort to maintain your warm, loving nature and don't become cold towards your husband because that could be one of the main attributes that attracted you to him in the first place.

4. Know: When to smile, when to say yes, when to say no, when to make a contribution, and when to keep quiet. REASON: Because this wins the affection of your husband.

What He Expects:

5. Your physical appearance, not just beauty, must be maintained, upgraded and updated, such as the latest lingerie, g-strings, tongs, sexual undies, bras, shorts, silky night gowns, see through baby doll, pajamas, short skirts at home revealing the body parts are all aspects of the sexual attraction.

6. Maintain your:

a. Neatness as well.

   b. Clean teeth and fresh breath. [both of you]

   c. A clean dress and clean underwear.

   d. PERSONAL HYGIENE: The hair under the armpit and the vulva, [private parts] must be well maintained, etc. (depending on cultures)

   e. You must smell fresh always. [both of you]

7. Don't get over involved in being busy with household chores, the children, work and other necessities to the detriment of caring for your man/husband.

8. Do everything in your power as a woman to keep your man/husband.

9. Give complete attention to your looks, put on the lipstick even at home, lip-gloss, lip-shine before bed, wear your hair up nicely always.

10. Always keep both yourself and the home clean and attractive.

11. Make it the kind of home that your husband always looks forward to coming to instead of driving past his house five times before coming home.

12. Create a warm, right, peaceful atmosphere for discussion, sharing, joy and laughter.

13. After a hard day's work find out what kind of day he had at work. It shows you are interested in what he does.

14. Respect your husband's privacy, without budging in or interfering or bombarding him with all sorts of questions; this makes him feel that you trust him.

15. Don't keep reminding him of, or repeating, rehearsing his past mistakes, failures or discrepancies. Don't bring back old, bad, painful memories of his past mistakes or shortcomings.

16. Don't nag at him. Such nagging behavior of a wife irritates the husband and makes him feel that he is of little value in her eyes and never gets anything right. It makes him ask himself questions such as, 'When will I ever get it right with Ms. Right or Ms. Perfect or Ms. Never Ever Makes A Mistake?' Or 'When will this Talkative or Nagging woman give me some peace and stop bringing up my past records from the book of 'CHRONICLES of husbands mistakes'?

17. Don't mess with your husband's ego; it means a

lot to every real man. Never ever ask degrading questions or make rude statements such as 'Are you a man' 'Do you have what it takes to be a man?' 'When men are speaking, you keep quiet.'

18. Don't keep reminding him of his shameful behavior. This may kill the loving spirit of the man. The best attitude for a wife is to forgive and forget, and make the man feel that in spite of what has happened he is still valued, respected, appreciated and loved.

19. Stand with and encourage your husband during rough, uncertain, difficult times of financial hardships, redundancy or unemployment without constantly being in his face or reminding him of it or lecturing him. Be understanding, discuss, pray and both of you believe God for a better and well-paid job or better still your own business.

20. Don't look down on your husband if you are more intelligent [with a higher intelligentsia quotient (IQ)] than he is or earn more than he does. Let him lead as the man, it builds his self-image and makes him want to live up to his responsibilities and the expectations of him as a man, a father, a husband, a king and a priest [the

prophet of his home].

21. Don't make statements like, 'It is my money, I will do what I want with it." No. Rather say, 'It is our money.' The two of you are now one. (Genesis 2:24)

22. Don't 'put on the trousers' at home. As much as possible, important decisions that affect the home and family should be taken by the husband, after detailed discussion with the wife and her input, concerns and suggestions have been taken under advisement.

23. Keep to time when you are going out with your husband. Don't make him honk the car horn before you come out or 'rev' the accelerator to get your attention and don't make him flare up or fume in anger in the car all the way to your destination because of your habitual lateness; and for heaven's sake, don't give excuses like, 'I need to dress up to look nice for you.' ADVICE: It is been proven that women, generally take longer to dress up than men. So, it's necessary, 'Pretty Lady' that you give yourself enough time to get ready by waking up early, be the first in the family to have your bath, finish your household chores early and dress up before he does. As you make the effort he'll give you a hand.

24. Genuinely appreciate your husbands' loving gestures, occasional gifts, no matter how big or small it is, and his attempts to assist in household chores such as cooking, tidying up the house, washing the dishes, running you a bath, ironing, helping with the children, etc.

25. Don't forget one of the major cardinal delights of a man - his food. The saying goes - 'A hungry man is an angry man.' Give your husband his food and he will listen to anything you have to say. Don't play games with him when it comes to his stomach and his food and don't delay in the preparation of his food. Someone once said, 'the way to a man's heart (to do some strange things for you) is through his stomach.' Cook his best meal, his favourite dish, make it very appealing, place it on a clean tray, with a kitchen towel and cutlery and a glass of cold or warm water or soft drink and bring it to him on a tray or call him over to the dinner table to eat if he prefers to eat there instead. You will score points always when you excel in this area. If you've already eaten before he came in, sit next to him on the dining table, keep him company, chat with him and caress him sometimes whilst he is eating without asking him to do anything for you. You will be scoring more points for what you need

from him later.

It is very true that every husband likes to enjoy the food prepared by his wife. Unfortunately, some wives tend to leave this all-important responsibility to their maids, au-pairs or house-helps. In certain homes, some wives leave all the cooking, washing of clothes, even sensitive clothes and items, such as pants and vests, cleaning the home, and even making the bed, to the maids or house-helps. This is not very wise. Reason being, if in some cases, the maid or house-help is able to perform these duties excellently, she wins the affection of the husband and then the wife becomes suspicious and jealous of this affection, and that marks the beginning of misunderstandings, tension and unhappiness in the home. It is essential therefore that a wife should know what household duties she should entrust to the maid or house-help and which sensitive ones she should undertake herself. Don't allow any house-help or any other woman to do anything that you as the wife must do. Take your place as a woman. You have only one shot at this marriage.

26. If you, the wife are the one who handles the financial resources of the family, learn how to manage it well, so that the family does not run

into hardship. Both of you must discover early in your relationship and take into consideration your strengths and weaknesses and the one who is more gifted in handling financial matters should handle the finances of the home working hand in hand with the other partner.

27. A wife must not be extravagant or a spendthrift or on e-bay or ordering online all the time. It is advisable in a marriage setting for both the husband and wife to pool their financial resources together for the future good of the family. It is advised that 80% of their joint income should be placed in a joint account to cater for major projects such as future major investments like a new house, car, education of children, etc. whilst reserving the 20% in equal amounts for pocket monies to cater for such minor necessities/purchases like socks, underpants, vests, tights, surprise gifts for birthdays, valentine's day, parents, anniversaries, surprise outings, etc. The advantage of pooling resources together is that it relieves the husband of the struggle and pressure of making ends meet on his own, enriches the relationship between the two and brings peace, stability, agreement, builds trust and harmony.

28. Both husband and wife must discuss fully and

reach an amicable agreement about any monies that must be given to family members such as parents or other relatives they have an obligation to take care of.

29. All forms of borrowing must first be discussed and decided on vis-à-vis the financial strength of the couple. No one should act unilaterally.

30. Be friendly, accommodating to the friends and relatives of your husband and handle them with great delicacy.

31. Be selective about your friends and which of them you allow to visit your home. It is said that keeping too many friends often leads to gossip and unnecessary comparison of wealth and standard of living. A woman's best friend should be her husband and a man's best friend should be his wife. Male friends can be even more dangerous as they cunningly try to woo the woman into having extra-marital relationships. Friends of the wife must as much as possible, become friends of the husband too. This may help eliminate unnecessary suspicion and mistrust – but it is always necessary to be diligent and guard against infidelity.

32. Be a real home-builder; be the best at this.

33. Don't starve your husband sexually; your body is his and his is yours. Do not defraud each other. (1 Corinthians 7:5)

34. By all means look good always – even when pregnant.

35. When the children start arriving, allocate your time wisely so your husband does not feel left out, sidelined, abandoned or used. The word is balance!

36. Don't let him be the one who is always initiating sexual relationships.

37. Don't let him fight for something that is natural.

38. Don't let him go looking for fuel at another station when he has his own fuel station at home.

39. Put a sign on your station saying 'Always open' and add an additional sign, 'PREMIUM OBTAIN'.

40. If you want your husband to be happy about sex with you, initiate sexual intercourse by being creative like choosing a special bulb which says, 'It will happen tonight'.

WHAT MEN WANT:

41. True companionship.

42. They look for health (physical, psychological, emotional, fiscal).

43. For the outward appearance of physical health, e.g. clear, bright eyes, a body not too overweight and not too underweight, clean lustrous hair, clean nails, clean body, few if any blemishes.

44. Someone beautiful but "beauty" is in the eye of the beholder."

45. A woman who is honest, who he can trust completely, who is not likely to sneak around and sleep around with other guys.

46. Someone with similar interests so they have something in common.

47. A woman who will make an effort to please him as he does too.

48. A woman who makes an effort to look her best. That is key!

49. An appreciation of the man's job.

50. Passion.

51. A woman whose ego isn't bigger than her hairstyle.

52. A partner for his life.

53. A partner for his soul.

54. Someone who is caring. All men want to be looked after.

55. Someone who has faith in him.

56. A woman who is strong yet scripturally submissive.

57. A woman who is strong but does not have an attitude. May have a far better job or earn more money than her husband but is forever humble, submissive and meek.

58. Someone who is not too loud.

59. Someone who won't nag him beyond reason.

60. A woman who challenges him and is full of the unexpected.

61. An interesting woman.

62. An intelligent woman.

63. A woman who is not dumb (mediocre intelligence

is fine).

64. A woman who is smart enough to grasp new concepts.

65. Someone artistic, innovative or creative.

66. A woman who can take care of herself without feeling that she has to compromise herself in a relationship.

67. Someone who suits their individual personality.

68. Some men like an aggressive woman.

69. Some men like the silent and reserved type.

70. Some men like one in-shape/athletic.

71. Interdependence, so that you trust and need each other.

72. One with a sense of humour.

73. A woman with a nice smile/laugh.

74. A positive personality.

75. A woman who is comfortable with her own sexuality.

76. Someone up for action or willing to get adventurous in the bedroom.

77. With a positive optimistic outlook.

78. A talent and passion in something worthwhile.

79. Men respect and want a woman who knows her own mind; women who are true to themselves.

80. Someone relaxed and confident.

81. A woman with a good soul.

82. A woman who has a great smile and loves to laugh and be herself but can also be intelligent and serious.

83. **Honest, timely, loving communication:** Honest communication is top priority for men. They want a woman who answers questions honestly, and perhaps even volunteers information. They want a woman who confidently asks for her wants and needs to be met. They want a woman who can see the truth and tell it like it is while communicating with kindness. Men want a woman who can communicate without being too critical, who cares about preserving his and her dignity. Women think men want them to be superficial, to keep quiet about their needs or wants, and never to ask for anything. Women think men believe them to be too needy and too sensitive, and that men simply want women to

get over it. Some women believe they do not have the permission to tell it like it is and that they will be rejected for speaking up.

A tip for women: Great men want and need straightforward, courageous communication without anger or criticism. One way to attract a great man and build a satisfying relationship is to learn how to communicate your truth and needs effectively.

84. **Self-sufficient, secure, confident women:** Men want a woman to choose them out of want rather than out of desperation — either materially or emotionally. Men need to be wanted and needed by their partners, but they want their partners to have a separate identity. Men want a woman to be active and independent, to have her own friends and interests. On the other hand, men treasure time spend with a loving partner.

Women think men don't want women to need them. Women think men do not need or appreciate time spent together as a couple. Women believe that showing a man that he is needed will turn him off and possibly make him run away.

A tip for women: Men want what women want

— a whole partner. One powerful way to attract a great man and build a vibrant relationship is to create a full, rewarding life for your own fulfillment.

85. **A manipulation-free relationship:** Men want no manipulation of any kind. They do not want to read their partner's mind or try to interpret signals. They do not want to be forced to move faster in a relationship than they are already. They do not want to be manipulated into taking all the blame for things gone wrong. They do not want to be on the receiving end of game playing.

    Some women think men want little or no communication, and the only way to get needs met is through manipulation. Some women think men either need or want to be reminded that the relationship needs to move forward. Some women think men don't want or value praise and acknowledgment, and so tend to only verbalize criticism.

    A tip for women: Men will not tolerate manipulation of any kind for any significant length of time. To attract a great man and build a wonderful relationship learn to ask without hesitation for what you want and need in every area of your life. Learn to be aware of his timing and his time-line. Learn how to acknowledge and bestow praise.

86. **Personal growth, development, personal responsibility and ownership:** Men want a partner who can laugh at herself and who has courage and strength. They want a woman who can see her part in relationship dynamics and own it. She has to be emotionally stable. Men want a woman who is developing herself personally, and who takes responsibility for her emotional experience.

Some women think men only want to have a good time and think men have no interest in developing and growing a relationship or developing and growing themselves. Some women think men want women who are super models and that they never consider whether a woman is emotionally mature, kind, supportive, or loving.

A tip for women: Men want women who are emotionally mature. Maturity does not mean lack of emotions. It does mean the ability to handle emotions responsibly. To attract a great man and build a long-term relationship, learn to take responsibility for your emotional experience and expression. Don't be moody too often - it turns men off!

87. **Fidelity and a commitment to the relationship:** Fidelity is an absolute must. In fact, men want a woman who does not have a "roaming eye" and who can wholeheartedly commit to the relationship. Many may define commitment as fidelity plus the willingness to work on the relationship — even when the going gets tough. Some women think that all men want is sex, and that men will leave a relationship for the next prettier face and some women think men cannot be trusted to be faithful and believe men do not want to work on a relationship; that when the going gets tough, they run.

   A tip for women: Here is great news for those women who are resigned to the myth that all men cheat: infidelity and "a roaming eye" are as distasteful to men as they are to women. Great men know how to build a wonderful relationship, and they know fidelity is the main ingredient.

88. **Men want women who know how men need to be treated:** Many women treat men in ways

that diminish their egos, making them feel inadequate by the things some women say and how they say it. Men would rather have more praise, more acknowledgment of what they do right, more acknowledgment that they are great men who are loved and appreciated.

Some women think men do not need them, do not value their opinion, their support, their praise and also think men do not care about many things important to women, which is why they criticize. Criticism is a way to verbalize resentment.

A tip for women: Most men want acknowledgment and appreciation from women. Learning to acknowledge instead of making your partner feel he is always or often wrong is one of the most powerful relationship survival tools available to you. So, use it wisely and use it very well.

89. A wise woman who does not tear her house down with her mouth and her hands. Proverbs 14:1, 'Every wise woman buildeth her house: but the foolish plucketh it down with her hands.'

90. A wife who will help her husband to have a stable and sound mind at home for a man confused

in his house will behave the same way in the office.

91. A genuine love-interest, i.e. they desire to love and they like being loved in return. This may surprise many women but men like to love and they like being loved in return. The problem is that many women come across as impassioned and cold. It is not easy to find a loving woman and it is very noticeable how many men try and hang on when they think they have found their Miss Right for life.

92. Men are seeking a woman who is attractive to them. Women may despair that men can be so shallow and that looks could matter so much but be careful. Men aren't necessarily looking for a catwalk model and many men don't like women who weigh 90lbs. But men do want a woman who takes pride in their appearance (though not excessively). Men are proud of having a woman who looks good and don't believe any man who says otherwise.

93. Men are looking for a trustworthy woman, someone they can have faith in and someone who will be there for them and someone in whom they can trust.

94. Men want to make a home eventually and are

looking for a woman who will be a willing sharer in home life. Women who are sociable with a lifestyle to match are attractive because they can be relied upon to keep the social diary running in a long term relationship.

95. Men are seeking women who are feminine, gentle and kind because deep down, the qualities that make a woman a great mother are an attraction in themselves. I am not suggesting that the man himself needs mothering, though some do but it is more the point that men seek the attributes in women that point to someone who would make a great mother to future offspring.

96. Men want women with a great sense of humor. Some women often come across as uptight or too bothered by too many small details. You will sometimes hear mention of a girl who is 'one of the boys'. What this means is that she is able to fit in with their humor and is sociable and fun to be with. Such women are extremely attractive to many men. Men want to have a good time and relax when not working and so their ideal partners are women who are able to do the same.

97. Men are looking for women who retain their femininity and are caring and kind.

98. Men want someone who is supportive. Many women are quick to criticize men in their behavior, career and set about trying to alter them and mould them. This is a crucial mistake. Men can be manipulated yes, but they see their partnerships as support systems. The best relationships work both ways in terms of support. Where a woman is not able or willing to give that encouragement or support and is too quick to criticize then she may lose her man.

99. Men don't like angry or moody women who shout, complain, murmur and nag all the time. They want a woman who can debate and converse and is able to discuss. Communication is king. A fiery passionate temperament may have made you interesting and challenging on day one. But by day 500 it holds no glory whatsoever.

100. Men love a motivationally challenging woman, someone who keeps them on their toes. Men are generally lazy in relationships once they feel they're in secure territory. When a man is challenged, he does something about it. If you want to keep your man interested, keep him challenged.

101. Men want a woman and a friend who they can share with and trust and be open with.

Commitment is not a one way street and therefore men are struggling to find the levels of commitment they found previously. But the need is still there.

102. Men don't want to be alone.

103. The fact is, a modern man is seeking a reliable, sexy, woman with whom he can have a long term relationship. They do seek self-respect from their partner even if they are not the primary breadwinner and they don't own the house they live in. While women become increasingly strong in their new roles in society, it is worth remembering that it takes, and always will take, two to tango.

104. **Men Want Confident Women:** As the statements from men and women on their likes and dislikes about each other differ, often relationships hit a rough patch. Most men want a woman who is comfortable with herself, is entertaining and a person who likes to take the new way. The women assume that men look for a certain kind of females and women try to be that kind of woman, some actually faking it. Men lose interest quite fast when they can see that the woman is not real.

105. **Men Attract Positive Women:** Rather than worry too much about what do men exactly want from women, she should concentrate on being herself and not trying to be someone she is not. One of the first things a man notices is the level of confidence in a woman. Women should be genuine: men respect and love that, his interests wanes as soon as he finds that the female is not what she is trying to be, or is not happy with herself. Men are attracted to women who are in complete control of themselves and are happy to be what she really is. In actual fact, men don't care about the flaws so much, men find women who don't care about flaws attractive. It attracts a man because he loves a challenge so he thinks it intriguing that a woman can be herself without any excuses for her frailties.

106. **Men Love Humorous Women:** So, drop that moodiness and blaming everything on your emotions. When considering what men exactly want from women it is important to know that men place a lot of importance on having a good time with their partners, men should enjoy the time they spend with the woman, this does not mean that they should have the same interests; it just means that the women should be able to laugh and be humorous and should be game

for some real fun. In short she should not be a spoilsport, she need not be a hitchhiker or superwoman, but she should be able to follow him and suggest to him some adventures like directing affairs 'in your office'. Be forward-looking and outgoing with a pleasant personality. Men really value that.

107. **Men Attract Kind Women:** The other criterion for men is that women should be caring and should have a lot of kindness. Men don't like being berated; it sets their testosterone going so they would see it as a challenge and fight it out. A small challenge is ok, but kicking a man when down is not done. Men love women who are happy and at peace with themselves and are assured about things in their life.

Men/Husbands like their woman/wife to have:

108. Good/sexy looks.

109. Warm smiles.

110. Sexy clothes – dress for him.

111. Glimpses of flesh even at home. (Stop wearing the sac all the time)

112. Sexual responsiveness.

113. Suggestion of sexual passion.

114. Admiration.

115. To Be: **A Wife/Mother who will:**

   a. Submit to her husband in all things. (Ephesians 5:22)

   b. Love her husband and children unconditionally. (Titus 2:4)

   c. Be a home builder.

What men don't want:
Rejection
Anger
Complaints
Criticism
Coldness
Moodiness
Degradation
Timetable on sex
Competition
Dishonesty
Infidelity
Rudeness
Control
Manipulation
Hurtful words that cut deep

Flattery
Nagging
Annoying habits

The real answer to what do men really want from women begins with who will be the most appropriate person they can partner with for life in a binding loving relationship to motivate each other selflessly towards destiny fulfilment involving a bit of adventure, a lot of honesty and confidence with a kind caring heart and a sense of humour backed by an unwavering support for each other's vision and passion that brings both of them fulfilment in life. Always keep in mind not to overdo things. Being overconfident, overbearing, manipulative, controlling, brutal or rude turns him off from you and he may drive past his house several times before he arrives home or even run away, so does faking or flattery when the truth is required. Above all be a virtuous woman! Let your virtuous biblical spirituality emanate in all you do and say and the how! **BE AND REMAIN HIS MAIN CHEER LEADER AND HIS KEY ALLY AND MOTIVATOR!**

Chapter Five

WOMEN BECOME MEN WHEN MEN STOP BEING MEN

In other words, women are forced to assume the responsible role of men only when men relinquish their required, life-changing and crucial responsibilities as men.

Malachi 4:5-6, "Behold, I will send you Elijah the prophet before the coming of the great and dreadful day of the LORD: And he shall turn the heart of the fathers to the children, and the heart of the children to their fathers, lest I come and smite the earth with a curse."

At the end of the Old Testament is a record of a fatherless problem.

Matthew 19:8, "He saith unto them, Moses because

of the hardness of your hearts suffered you to put away your wives: but from the beginning it was not so."

So, we need to go back, examine and take our clue from what His original purpose and intention for man and relationships was. That is the only way we can experience maximum results and get the most and best out of man and our relationships.

God's original intention for man: 1 Corinthians 11:7-9; Genesis 1:26; 2:18–25; Proverbs 12:4

'Being male is by birth; but being a man is by choice.' – Myles Munroe.

You must choose to be a man and function as a man. 'Men must be men, not sissies making ninnies of themselves.' - A quote in the 'Parent Trap.'

QUOTE: Being a man is not having a beard, big flashy car, a moustache, side burns, muscles, big house or a cigarette. Being a man involves responsibilities, i.e. taking on and fulfilling responsibilities is what makes you a man. The reason God made a woman was because the man had no companion, partner or helpmeet. So, a **woman was made for and because of man.** Women exist because of men and women must remain and function as women and men must take up their rightful responsible masculine role as men and remain men for there to be order, peace, security, and stability.

There is the need for us to return to divine order – God's order of doing things. Reason being: Churches and nations are made out of the family. Nations are made out of people. A man confused in his house will behave the same way in the office. What you are in the house is what you should be in the office.

GOD EXPECTS CERTAIN THINGS OF US AS MEN: A man has five main roles and must be, must function and succeed in all these 5 areas. A man must be a:

1. Man

2. Husband

3. Father

4. Priest

5. King

Your time must be well allocated to fulfil these roles. **As a Man,** you are to:

a. Guide, guard and govern – you must bring direction.

b. Be fruitful, multiply, replenish, subdue, take charge and exercise absolute dominion. (Genesis 1:26-28; 18:19)

c. Men should not allow their parents to tell them what to do in their Christian walk or marriage or wait till they've consulted with them before taking crucial decisions in their homes.

d. Take charge, command, be decisive, stable, defenders, rule well your home and be protectors of the household. (James 1:5-8)

e. Put God first, family second and ministry or work third.

f. Be visionary and have a clear sense of direction, purpose, responsibility, commitment and leadership. Vision and leadership must come primarily from the man, such as 'where are we heading; in what direction?' Jesus at the age 12 knew what He was about – He knew His assignment. John 4:34 says in response to a question about what he would have to eat, Jesus' reply was, 'My meat is to do the will of Him that sent me and to finish it.' May you discover, know, begin to walk in and fulfil your divine assignment early in life – it brings focus.

g. Provide for the family, working within reason.

h. We must never be intimidated by the success of our

wives or those we train who are coming up behind us. The head is always the head and the body with its parts always remains the body, so we are in charge – church structure. Take the lead and apply for a council flat or house if living in the UK as a man.

i. Be creative, inventive in securing your family and your future, plan ahead of time. You need sight, insight, foresight and far-sight to foresee things ahead of time and make provision for them. You must never be taken by surprise. **Prepare for your future by preparing in the summer for winter; prepare today in great anticipation of a bright and better tomorrow** not only for you but for your family, community, church, city, nation, nations and generations yet unborn. So, when the time comes you just walk in and possess. (**Go to the ant and learn from him how to maximize times and seasons – Proverbs 6:6-11**) WINTER [October-December]; SPRING [January-March], AUTUMN [April-June]; SUMMER [July-September]

j. CRUCIAL ADVICE: Everyone that is responsible for another person owes that person a leadership responsibility because you are influencing people daily with or without walls. Every parent is a leader leading their family with Grace [favour and ability - skill in parenting] or into disgrace and shame. Don't start a family without skill or the know-how of parenting - you delay, derail, experiment with or will destroy destinies because experience is not the best teacher as the traditionalists believe. Because, everything rises and falls on leadership, everything also boils down to who is leading that family, that organisation, that church, that department, that business, that city or that nation.

The future of this nation will be determined by parents, how you raise, train your children, what you feed their minds - your example, whether you the man come to church and are actively involved or you tell them they should go with their mother and you stay at home, the principles you live by, where it has its origin i.e. your friends, the pub, on the job, from your uncle, the way you were raised, do you live by satanic principles or God's principles. Who and what leads the father is what the wife and mother and children will be led by except the wife is determined to serve God irrespective if the man is not taking his place.

LEADERSHIP MATTERS: Leadership is crucial – as the head of the family [man/husband/father/priest/king] goes, so does the wife and the children and that is why Proverbs 14:34, says, 'Righteousness exalts a nation: but sin is a reproach to any people.'

The word **exalt** from the 15th century - Latin word exaltare, literally means:

i. 'to put up high'

ii. to promote: to raise somebody or something in rank, position, or esteem (formal) like exalted to the rank of major

iii. praise: to praise or worship somebody or something

iv. intensify: to increase the intensity or effect of something

v. stimulate: to stimulate a mental quality or faculty (archaic)

vi. raise: to raise somebody or something physically (archaic)

Reproach on the other hand means disgrace somebody or something: to bring disgrace upon somebody or something.

From the above definitions we conclude that who heads or who leads a family, an organisation, church, ministry, football club, business, city or a nation determines to a large extent whether that organisation, family or church is moving forward, is put up high, is praised, is intensified in its effectiveness, is stimulated is raised, is promoted or is brought down low, disgraced and brought to shame. That's why the bible warns every family, people and nation in Ecclesiastes 10:16, 'Woe to thee, O land, when thy king [leader] is a child, and thy princes eat in the morning!'

REASON: Galatians 4:1 says, 'Now I say, That the heir, as long as he is a child, differeth nothing from a servant, though he be lord of all;'

Woe meaning: unfortunate happening: a serious affliction or misfortune.

Grief: grief or distress resulting from a serious affliction or misfortune.

- Every father or mother is a leader leading their children either into destruction or into distinction.

Every head of the family, every father is the leader of his family driving the family vehicle with his wife, his children and his entire household. So, his skillfulness and influence at the steering wheel of life determines the destiny of his home. If he drives rough and ends up in prison or dies, he leaves his family as destitutes. If I steal money or mismanage funds and end up in prison or if I die prematurely, God forbid, both of which will never happen, I know without a shadow of doubt that there is no family member, distant or close or any human being dead or alive who will rise up to assume or take good or even bad care of my family except God intervenes. There is No family member. So I cannot afford as the man and head of my family to live a reckless life. There is only one Hutton-Wood family from my loins, the first chosen by God; there is no one in my family called Hutton-Wood; I am the only one and God is counting on me - it is a privilege.

ITS NOT A RIGHT BUT A PRIVILEGE just like my father in the Lord was told by God, 'It is a privilege you have to lead this church; if you abuse this privilege, there are hundreds better than you waiting at the door to come in.' So, I cannot afford to teach something different other than what He's put in my mouth and in the way that will make maximum impact. The magnitude i.e. the seriousness of the assignment and message is what dictates our passion.

Proverbs 13:22, 'A good man leaveth an inheritance to his children's children: and the wealth of the sinner is laid up for the just.'

Have you written a will? Will your family be adequately provided for, not averagely provided for, but adequately provided for in case of an eventuality; i.e. if something happens to you or God decides you've finished your job on the earth, so come home. If you leave now, will the mortgage be paid off still with loads of money to spare or will they depend on the state or go round begging? Abraham made provision even unto our generation and beyond. Levi tithed in his great-grandfather Abraham. What Abraham did is what the 12 tribes of Israel in the physical land of Israel in the Middle East i.e. physical Israel spread across the earth and spiritual Israel [us] are enjoying now. One man's obedience through a walk of faith is what has qualified us for Abraham's blessings through acceptance of Christ, tithing and obedience.

MEN AND FATHERS - God has appointed us as leaders in our homes.

REMEMBER the following sayings:

- Real Leaders Devote uninterrupted chunks of time to the most important people in their life.

- Leaders always Remember: it's quantity of time at home, and quality of time at work, that counts.

- Avoid making decisions on matters that don't need decisions. If it is not necessary to decide, it is necessary not to decide.

- Build wisdom and confidence in others by forcing them to think and decide for themselves.

So man, husband, father, lead the family; don't follow the wife. Take the lead; your wife must follow you, the man and children follow both of you, the parents. Train up a child [track the child] in the way he should go not the way they want to go and when they grow up, they will not depart from it. If there is no man in the house then the woman must lead - God is your husband - be addicted to this book and lead your family by this book - Joshua 1:8. But where the man is at home, the wife must follow her Christian, kingdom-minded husband as he follows and takes instructions from God - The Ultimate Leader and the man of God [God's representative - Hosea 12:13; 2 Chronicles 20:20b] Hold on to his apron as he holds on to God and honours God not despises the man of God; and children you hold on to mama's apron as she holds on to Godly papa's aprons strings as he holds on to God and the man of God sent from God and it will be well with you all and you will live long on the earth (Ephesians 6:1-3). IF GOD IS NOT LEADING THAT FAMILY, YOU ARE LEADING YOURSELF and YOU ARE at the mercy of the elements of this world and are HEADED FOR DOOM OR DISGRACE!

So, mama holds on to dad and children hold on to mama and obey what papa heard from God and his word. That is what the family must look like - that's what train - track the child in Proverbs 22:6 means. That is the only way to make it big and become influential and impactful in life and for generations to come. John D. Rockefeller was a dangerously rich and wealthy man and he was a tither and passed his legacy on just like Conrad Hilton to his children and Rockefeller's foundation still exists today and is still running very strong. Bill Gates gives 10% of his earnings to charities every year, 10% yet some born again Christians are robbers. Hebrews 7 says you are being marked absent or present because of your tithe in heaven so when you need something, the angels can look in the tithe register and see if you qualify to withdraw from your heavenly account or whether you have anything there to write a cheque against. Hebrews 7:8 confirms this: 'And here men that die receive tithes; but there he [JESUS our High Priest] receiveth them, of whom it is witnessed that he liveth.'

SOME PEOPLE ARE ASKING GOD FOR CERTAIN THINGS THEY HAVE NO BUSINESS ASKING FOR. Abraham your father in the faith whose songs you sing about was a tither, so if you want to enjoy Abraham's blessing, then dedicate yourself to tithing consistently. Don't touch God's money. The man should take the lead for the wife and family to follow. Don't argue with your wife or wife to be about the tithe; you are not leading if you do that. So read, learn, have an insatiable thirst for knowledge in your area of expertise, calling, vocation or profession. Be very informed about life and about people. Don't trust everyone.

PRIORITISE: Out of 100%, put God first with 40% then 30% allocated in equal quantity for the family and ministry/profession/vocation in second and third place respectively. Don't let any area suffer at the expense of the other. Live a very balanced and very selective life about who you call your friends, comrades or associates; watch and vet who you allow into your inner circle. Be extremely selective because not everyone or just anyone must qualify to be in your inner circle or have your phone number - spiritually and physically or give you advise. He who says, 'Leave your wife after a disagreement' is believing God for her.

Be an ardent observer of Psalm 1:1-3 and 1 Corinthians 15:33. Live by this scripture daily. Men, don't trust that woman's smile and short skirt, she's lying. I am telling you she's lying; she's an agent of Satan; she will floor you and dump you like a sack of potatoes. And woman, don't trust that smooth-talking man; discern. He only wants one thing and you know what that one thing is; so, decide for yourself - preserve it! And youth don't run into anything that will delay you, derail you or slow you down in your academic life or for life. Young boys who never had a father figure, role model or mentor at home we say we are very proud of you and you can make it; and young girls who never had a real dad at home to tuck you into bed, date you, love you, give you flowers, tell you he loves you or those who had an ignorant, ineffective or absent father and so you lacked affection and want someone to tell you, you are beautiful and they love you, I ask you to forgive your father, be healed and I stand in the gap as God's representative, and assure you that you are very beautiful, glamorous, pretty and God loves you so much and I love you too. Don't sell yourself cheap or short - study, make something great out of your life till you grow up and through prayer, divine direction, discernment, wisdom, planning, right choices, a deep understanding of love [Agape, Storge, Phileo, Eros] and the institution of marriage we WILL GIVE YOU AWAY gloriously and be there for you. Till then, young men and women, put God first in everything, get involved in your churches, be mentored, study, remain humble and teachable, research, learn, read, be the best - study to show yourself approved as the sought-after - the nurse, the accountant, the doctor, the teacher, the lecturer, the governor, the preacher, the business man or woman, the hotel magnate, the man or woman of the year, the actress, the TV station owner, the shipping tycoon, the airline tycoon, the mayor; the film director, the next Stephen Spielberg, the choreographer, the African or Caribbean Bill Gates, the politician, not the one coming to make money at the expense of the nation; the banker or bank manager, not the crook who duped people and placed the monies in Swiss accounts, the lawyer, not the one that gets pedophiles and murderers off the hook with a technicality or loophole in the law and rather become who God destined you to be for Deuteronomy 28 states you are the head and not the tail.

Church, let's take over the schools, colleges, universities, banks, cities, colleges, hospitals, TV stations, create new films that promote what we believe. Let's tell our vision on TV, for that is what television is - tell a vision [tell your vision]. If we don't seek first the kingdom, stand with our churches with our time, energies, gifts, talents, finances, resources and prayer to buy and own television stations and put out our programs they will keep showing us what they want us to see and be. Hollywood will tell us what family life should be; governments will pass laws and dictate to us that Adam and Steve are the ideal couple instead of Adam and Eve. MTV will play 24/7 what music our children should sing and the way they should dress and as if that is not bad enough CNN will fill our screen every hour with depressing news about murders, terrorism, floods, rapes, etc. around the world.

LISTEN: Church is not about just coming and hearing some songs and word and announcements and go home and rest. NO, a capital no! It's about fellowship, training, impartation, acquiring knowledge, getting wisdom and understanding to go and minister. Influence! Influence! Impact! Impact! Reconstructing a generation by Raising a new generation of leaders with a generationally-building mindset, to repair the old waste cities! We are course-charters, trail-blazers, pathfinders who are out to chat the course, blaze a trail, find the new path for the next generation, not a me alone, my family only mindset. We have a mission to set in order the things that are out of order. Changing society and influencing nations - that is what church is about and it starts with the family. Everything rises and/or falls on leadership out there or at home. That is why leadership is so important. Don't just get married or give birth to children, leaders! Your examples are being observed and acted on by others. Actors and actresses listen to me as well! People are following your example in dressing and in behaviour; so, conduct yourselves appropriately, etc.

- LEADERS: LISTEN TO GOD & THE MEN OF GOD & OBEY & OBSERVE GOD'S WORD THEY PREACH TO YOU.

- IF THE LEADERS GET IT RIGHT, THE FOLLOWERS WILL GET IT RIGHT and that's why we as leaders of churches cannot afford to make the mistakes of the previous regimes or generations either in word, indeed, in character or attitudes; our children in church are watching us, learning from us, taking their clues from us and the world is watching and waiting for us. Romans 8:19, 'For the earnest expectation of the creature waiteth for the manifestation of the sons of God.'

WARNING TO THE UNIVERSAL CHURCH OF GOD: Stop fighting and bickering or in competition with one another and conferring titles on yourselves, bothered about what they call you or how they see you instead of winning souls and seeing to the welfare of the members. Who cares what you are called or what somebody thinks about you; it's irrelevant, please God, do the word, do the work, win souls, take care of people out there and raise leaders! Be about the master's business.

CHURCH & FAMILY INTERWOVEN: The church is made up of families so, if the families get it right from doing the principles of the word, the church will get it right and vice versa for the world to learn from and be influenced by. IF THE CHURCH made up of families get it right, then as we go into society which is waiting for us as solution-providers and role-models the society will be influenced by what we know and do and they will get it right. Until the church gets it right and influences society, society will continue to deteriorate. THE ONLY HOPE FOR THE WORLD, IS THE CHURCH and the leaders that are coming out of those churches.

We won't change the world just by the word of mouth or sitting in our corner; we must break into every sphere of life and not be dominated or dictated to by the world but we aiming for and rising up in our work places into positions of prominence, influence and power to promoting our beliefs and aspirations enforcing the principles of God's kingdom here on the earth; if not society will deteriorate.

Dr. Myles Munroe said if he was offered the position of Prime Minister in his nation, Bahamas, it will be too small a position for him to accept because as a result of him being a very well-informed pastor, educator, advisor, lecturer, international conference speaker, consultant, businessman, best-selling author, through tertiary training [I.e. school, college, university and ongoing personal development] he now influences political leaders of first, second and third world countries such as, governors, senators, congressmen, heads of state, parliamentarians, presidents of nations all around the world plus chief executives, ministers, pastors, bishops, etc. That is what we are called to do. That is what the church is here for. IMPACT! INFLUENCE! IMPACT! INFLUENCE! Read the Bible, my books, resource materials, books of such people and listen to my leadership CDS, WATCH THE DVDs and that of such people and you can understand what God has called you to be and do and a correct understanding of who you really are will give you a proper balance for your head when God promotes you. Ability will take you to the top but only character traits such as faithfulness, honesty, integrity and loyalty can keep you at the top. So get skill plus character.

As a Husband: (Ephesians 5:25-33; 1 Peter 3:7)

- You must love and care for your wife. (Ephesians 5:23)

- If you know how to treat your woman, she'll build you up wherever you are; her heart will be with you to lift you up to the heights. (Proverbs 31) If not she'll pull you down quick. Women can either make you or break you.

- The bodies of women are built for affection, love and comfort.

- The bodies of men are built to provide strength, warmth (feet-warming of your wife's cold feet in bed) and security.

- Show your wife affection, love, shower her with praises, appreciate her and make boast of her in the Lord – her cooking, her looks, etc.

- When you go out in the field, your wife's heart must be out there with you.

- When there is a choice between wealth, riches,

property and the husband's affection and love, a real woman will choose the latter except some weird women who will not even let you give a penny to those in need.

- The only language a woman understands is love and affection. That is why you see very pretty women going out with a not so gorgeous or handsome man. Why? Because the man has been able to sweep her off her feet with a great show of affection; that is – love, affection and attention is at work.

- Set aside quality time for your wife – put the children to bed together or divide the work among you and take a break together sometimes.

- Date her every week or two weeks and have a honey moon every six months. [Refer to previous chapters and get a copy of my book: 101 Tips for a great marriage from our bookshop or our website www.houseofjudah.org.uk]

As a Father, we have great responsibilities.

Proverbs 22:6, 'Train up a child in the way he should go: and when he is old, he will not depart from it.'

QUOTE: from (U.S. News and world report, February, 27, 1995)

"Dad is destiny." "A biological father's presence

in the family will determine a child's success and happiness."

"Fatherlessness is the most destructive trend of our generation," argues David Blakenhorn, author of the provocative book, Fatherless America: Confronting our most urgent social problem.

From the preface of The Principle of Fatherhood by Myles Munroe:

"The absence of fathers is linked to most social nightmares-from boys with guns to girls with babies. No welfare reform can cut poverty as thoroughly as a two-parent family. Some 46% of children in single mother families live below the poverty line, compared with 8% of those with two parents. Raising marriage rates will do far more to fight crime than building prisons or putting more cops on the streets. Studies show that only 43% of state prison inmates grew up with both parents and that a missing father is a better predictor of criminal activity than race or poverty. Having both parents in the home is a better antidote to teen pregnancy than handing out condoms and birth control pills."

Also in a survey done by U.S, News and world report, 71% of those surveyed said, "It is very important for every child to have his or her father living at home," and nearly 8 out of 10 thought that both fathers and mothers should spend more time with their children. Some 58% said it should be harder for couples with children to get a divorce.

"Divorce can increase an adult's happiness, but it is devastating to a child," says psychologist Judith Wallerstein, who has studied her child clients since 1971.

In closing, there is further evidence to show that there are critical emotional and psychological needs that only a male can provide, just as there are specific needs only the female is designed to meet. Therefore the absence of either has an effect on development, despite the seemingly normal development and function of the human family.

So, as Fathers: we have a responsibility to:

- Tend, guard, guide and govern. Give direction, protect, defend, provide for the family and spend quality time with them. (Psalm 91)

- Train, track the child (Genesis 17:2,4,7; 18:19; Proverbs 13:24; 22:6; Isaiah 54:13,14; Ephesians 6:4; 1 Timothy 5:8)

- Nations and society is made out of the family; the stronger the families the stronger the nation. Scripture says, 'Righteousness exalts a nation but sin is a reproach to every nation.' One of the major reasons why we have a weak nation morally and spiritually is because the men have stopped being men by moving house, abandoning their unique God-given responsibility of the training and raising of children, leaving them to be raised and trained by the mothers, school teachers, Sunday school teachers, nannies, maid servants and Pastors. It is not the job or responsibility of Pastors to teach your child to respect his/her parents. It is the responsibility of the parents – the father and mother. If your child does not respect, the fault is from the home not the church. Scripture exhorts us, fathers to train up a child in the way **he should go**, [not the way they want to go] and when they grow up they would not depart from it. We must train children to call adults not by their first names but by their titles, function or position of authority and by their office in life - that is respect.

- When women are left to raise, train and care for children alone or on their own, the children tend to be at the mercy of the elements of this world, but for the grace of God.

- Women don't have seed – women cannot give birth without the man's seed. God has given women the singular grace and endowment to do us the honour of using this great heavenly, remarkable, distinct, unique, invaluable gift of the womb to carry our seed.

- It is the responsibility of the father to train the child. Children bear the name of the father and not the name of the mother because men were put in charge or made responsible. When God came into the garden to find out what was going on, he called out and asked, "Adam where art thou?"Not Eve because he made the man responsible for the garden. (Genesis 3:9) Women reproduce after the man's kind, they can't be pregnant without a man's seed. Women are made for the man – not vice versa. (1 Corinthians 11:8-9)

- Men take up your responsibilities and train your children.

- Balance discipline with a show of love, attention and interest in what your children do and their interests. Go to their school functions, sports games, drama, music, parents evening, etc. Participate and show keen interest. Buy them things that will help them to function better, excel and turn out better in life such as computers, laptops, etc.

- Women allow the men to be men and they'll allow you to be women; don't attempt to be who you're not. Don't abuse your purpose and bring chaos to the home.

- Divisions, strife and misunderstandings in churches are as a result of strife, divisions and misunderstandings at home. Everyone must find, know and function in their respective roles.

- The wife must be in subjection to her own husband, not to someone else's husband. They should be kept in subjection, not to dominate their husbands.

- Women must see to it that they reverence their husbands no matter who they are. Wives must submit to their husbands as long as it's not in violation of God's commandments. If it's not in line with God's word, God's word must have the final authority. Don't do it.

- Men are usually very hard on the firstborns and sometimes those that come after especially the lastborns get away with anything.

- Tell your son how handsome, clever and great he is. Tell him how proud you are of him and send him text messages expressing all this occasionally. Take him out for manly activities like sports, things he likes doing. It enables them grow up with self-confidence, acceptance and worth.

- Show your daughter love and affection as you are her first sweet heart so they don't grow up to fall for men below their capacity because they showed them more attention than you did. When they needed your warm hands to tuck them into bed, your hands were busy signing cheques or building more houses or attending more meetings. Date her, take her out for a meal sometimes, buy her gifts, flowers, shower her with praises, comment her on her looks, tell her how proud you are of her and show them by words, text messages and deeds who, how and what a real husband ought to be.

- Live a balanced life so as to fulfil all the five roles well. Your children will remember everything, all the invaluable deposits and contributions you made, your presence in their upbringing as they grew up or the lack of it. Children learn more by your example than by what you say or keep saying. They are the ones who will testify of you as to whether you were a good father or not. I trust that your testimony will read that you were great and you left an inheritance for your children's children as scripture requires.

- Men, take your sons to the field to preach, etc. Let them see you at work i.e. what you do. E.g. our children used to go with us, distributing tracts, leaflets house to house; today they are actively involved in ministry with us. These children learn a lot by observation: how daddy treats mummy, how mummy treats and respects or disrespects daddy. That is what they'll learn and do when they are married. Don't ever come to church without your children. What they learn to do now, they'll always do when they grow up. They can tell what is a priority to their parents and what isn't. Tithing or robbing God; swearing or decent conversation at home; good telephone ministry of counselling and encouragement or gossiping on the phone; peace or war at home; real or fake – same in church and at home or wild as a tiger at home and humble as a dove in church, etc. They see; they notice because charity begins at home. A child who misbehaves in church misbehaves at home; it's the parent's responsibility to train/track that child.

- Instil in your children your vision and dream for your family – your principles. What you stand for and what you won't tolerate.

***Boys learn to be men from their fathers and Girls learn to be women from their mothers.** So, what impression of a man are you giving to your son, dad, and what impression of a woman are you giving to your daughter, mum?

- Don't argue or show misunderstanding before or in front of your children. Go and hold 'conference' in the privacy and quietness of your bedroom.

- When your children come and ask you for something, always discuss the subject together with your wife before giving your children your conclusion so the decision you make is clear to your children as having been decided on by both of you, instead of just by you. It shows unity and brings respect and it also tells the child daddy won't do anything without consulting mum so I can't side them against each other by saying mum said yes but dad said no or vice versa.

- Success without a successor is failure. What we are teaching our children today is not only for our children but the future leaders of our nation and other nations (Acts 1:8; Psalm 2:8). **We are either raising up and training a weak nation or a strong nation.**

- A lot of men have acquired names, property and wealth but not children. You cannot call your boy my son if you've not being a father to him by playing that role in his life. A father is a father who is present, active and involved in the child's life and upbringing not an absentee father. Giving birth to a child doesn't make you a father. Being present to fulfil your role daily as a father is what makes you a father.

- Make time to take the family on holidays and outings.

- Many children of certain pastors have refused to serve God and accept God's call on their lives because their father was always concerned about others at the detriment of their family. We must fulfil both. There is no point in saving the whole world and losing your family. Remember scripture says he who does not take care of his own family is worse than an infidel. A pastor's first congregation is his wife and children.

Fathers show the children the way, the direction to follow. (John 14:6)

- Moral and spiritual leadership is the responsibility of fathers.

- Some succeed as men [taking charge], as husbands but fail as fathers. That shall not be our portion!

YOU MUST BECOME THE HUSBAND YOUR DAUGHTER WOULD WANT TO MARRY [IN A FUTURE HUSBAND] AND THE FATHER YOUR SON WOULD WANT TO BE [TO HIS CHILDREN]!

***The Father as a disciplinarian

Fathers have the responsibility of disciplining the children. Discipline is not punishment. Discipline takes teaching to another level; it is one thing to teach a child but correction and further instruction helps to shape a child's character. Discipline therefore is training; it is not punishment. Fathers are supposed to instruct their children not leave the disciplining of the children to women. (Ephesians 6:4, Genesis 2:5, 15, 18) God loves to cultivate. Discipline must be rendered in love not out of anger. (Colossians 3:21)

- God the Father disciplines us, and godly fathers like God discipline their children. Fathers train and discipline their children by having them follow their example. (Hebrews 12:5-10)

- A good father follows the example of the Father and teaches his offspring to follow him. A godly father leads everyone following him to the Father. Jesus did that to his disciples.

As a PRIEST of the home:

- Men are supposed to give moral and spiritual direction and insist on obedience to God's word. (Genesis 2:15-17; 3:9; Psalm 91)

- The man is to protect, guard and defend the house, home, family and keep away any alien and contrary spirits. God said, 'Adam, my man, where art thou?' He addressed him because He was the one whom God put in charge.

- You are to intercede and represent God before your family.

- You must buy into the mind of God concerning your family – their future, direction, purpose, prayer requests, needs, wants, supplies, etc. – Isaac & Rebecca

- Many men are sitting in their lazy chairs, sleeping whilst their wives are waking up to pray or driving them to study God's word or come to church; this ought not to be – it is out of order. That's why we have a weak and immoral society because the men are not functioning as men. They have relinquished their responsibilities as men. Men, it is time to arise and shine, rise up, take your place for your light has come (Isaiah 60) wake up, men!

- Teach your child how to pray and why. Take them to church. Live the word before them. Talk of the word on the dining table. Instil them with God's principles. The head must always play the role of the head in every way.

As a King: (Revelation 1:6)

- You rule, command, administer judgment in mercy.

- You must be decisive, not in-decisive!

- You must be stable in all your ways. (James 1:5-8; Genesis 18:19; 1 Timothy 3:5)

- You are the one on whom the woman leans for comfort, encouragement, direction, praise, purpose, direction and vision.

- You must be firm, confident in your beliefs, your convictions and decisions. Have a clear-cut sense of direction and conviction.

- Single women. This is the kind of man you need in your life - pray him in, wait patiently for him, pray in this character formation and principles.

For those of you who are already married, wives: this is the husband you need. Help your husband become a truly godly man, husband, father, priest and king.

(Get my books: '200 questions you must ask before you say 'I DO'' and '101 **Tips for a Great Marriage' from our website www.houseofjudah.org.uk**

RELATIONSHIPS SEMINAR

FOUR SEASONS OF MARRIAGE EXERCISE:

At Every Point in Time in your marriage, you are either in **SPRING, SUMMER, WINTER OR FALL [AUTUMN]**. **So,** TICK WHICH ONE IS APPLICABLE TO WHERE YOU ARE IN YOUR MARRIAGE NOW SO YOU KNOW WHAT TO IMPROVE OR KEEP DOING.

MARRIAGE RELATIONSHIPS INDICATOR
HUSBAND INDICATOR CHART

1. a. Discouraging   b. Exciting   c. Satisfying   d. Uncertain

2. a. Hopeless   b. Happy   c. Peaceful   d. Confusing

3. a. Empty   b. Hopeful   c. Committed   d. Stressful

4. a. Harsh   b. Nurturing   c. Secure   d. Frustrating

5. a. Resentful   b. Open   c. Trusting   d. Tired

6. a. Destructive   b. Fresh   c. Relaxed   d. Distant

7. a. Rejection   b. Anticipation   c. Appreciation   d. Apprehension

8. a. Tension   b. Sharing   c. Honest   d. Drifting

9. a. Give up   b. Making Plans   c. Teamwork   d. Apathetic

10. a. Critical   b. Caring   c. Connected   d. Concerned

11. a. Angry   b. Joyful   c. Understanding   d. Burned Out

12. a. Disappointed   b. Optimistic   c. Comfortable   d. Neglectful

13. a. Untrusting   b. Tender   c. Supportive   d. Afraid

14. a. Withdrawn   b. Growing   c. Attached   d. Detached

15. a. Cold   b. Alive   c. Content   d. Prideful

16. a. Unforgiving   b. Willing to change   c. Overlook flaws   d. Growing apart

-      -   -   -

Column 1 Total   Column 2 Total   Column 3 Total   Column 4 Total

_____   _____   _____   _____

RELATIONSHIPS SEMINAR

FOUR SEASONS OF MARRIAGE EXERCISE:

At Every Point in Time in your marriage, you are either in **SPRING, SUMMER, WINTER OR FALL [AUTUMN]. So,** TICK WHICH ONE IS APPLICABLE TO WHERE YOU ARE IN YOUR MARRIAGE NOW SO YOU KNOW WHAT TO IMPROVE OR KEEP DOING.

MARRIAGE RELATIONSHIPS INDICATOR
WIFE INDICATOR CHART

1. a. Discouraging   b. Exciting   c. Satisfying   d. Uncertain
2. a. Hopeless   b. Happy   c. Peaceful   d. Confusing
3. a. Empty   b. Hopeful   c. Committed   d. Stressful
4. a. Harsh   b. Nurturing   c. Secure   d. Frustrating
5. a. Resentful   b. Open   c. Trusting   d. Tired
6. a. Destructive   b. Fresh   c. Relaxed   d. Distant
7. a. Rejection   b. Anticipation   c. Appreciation   d. Apprehension
8. a. Tension   b. Sharing   c. Honest   d. Drifting
9. a. Give up   b. Making Plans   c. Teamwork   d. Apathetic
10. a. Critical   b. Caring   c. Connected   d. Concerned
11. a. Angry   b. Joyful   c. Understanding   d. Burned Out
12. a. Disappointed   b. Optimistic   c. Comfortable   d. Neglectful
13. a. Untrusting   b. Tender   c. Supportive   d. Afraid
14. a. Withdrawn   b. Growing   c. Attached   d. Detached
15. a. Cold   b. Alive   c. Content   d. Prideful
16. a. Unforgiving   b. Willing to change   c. Overlook flaws   d. Growing apart

Column 1 Total   Column 2 Total   Column 3 Total   Column 4 Total

_____   _____   _____   _____

MARRIAGE JOKES TO LAUGH OFF FROM E-MAILS!

Marriage SWEET Jokes!!!!!!!!!!!!! !!!!!!!!!

Wife: 'What are you doing?'
Husband: 'Nothing.'
Wife: 'Nothing...? You've been reading our marriage certificate for an hour.'
Husband: 'I was looking for the expiry date.'

Wife: 'Do you want dinner?'
Husband: 'Sure! What are my choices?'
Wife: 'Yes or no.'

Wife: 'You always carry my photo in your wallet...... Why?'
Husband: 'When there is a problem, no matter how great, I look at your picture and the problem disappears.'
Wife: 'You see how miraculous and powerful I am for you?'
Husband: 'Yes! I see your picture and ask myself what other problem can there be greater than this one?'

Stress Reliever: Girl: 'When we get married, I want to share all your worries, troubles and lighten your burden.' Boy: 'It's very kind of you, darling, but I don't have any worries or troubles.' Girl: 'Well that's because we aren't married yet.'

A newly married man asked his wife, 'Would you have married me if my father hadn't left me a fortune?' 'Honey, the woman replied sweetly, 'I'd have married you, NO MATTER WHO LEFT YOU A FORTUNE!'

Girl to her boyfriend: 'One kiss and I'll be yours forever.' The guy replies: 'Thanks for the early warning.'

A wife asked her husband: 'What do you like most in me, my pretty face or my sexy body?' He looked at her from head to toe and replied: 'I like your sense of humour!'

Husbands are husbands: A man was sitting reading his papers when his wife hit him round the head with a frying pan. 'What was that for?' the man asked. The wife replied, 'That was for the piece of paper with the name Jenny on it that I found in your pants pocket'. The man then said 'When I was at the races last week Jenny was the name of the horse I bet on'

The wife apologized and went on with the housework. Three days later the man was watching TV when his wife bashes him on the head with an even bigger frying pan, knocking him unconscious. Upon re-gaining consciousness the man asked why she had hit him again. Wife replied: 'Your Horse phoned!!!' **Give me a sense of humour, Lord. Give me the grace to see a joke, to get some humour out of life. Please laugh it off! Thank you!**

HUSBAND SHOPPING STORE

A store that sells husbands has just opened in Windhoek, where a woman may go to choose a husband. Among the instructions at the entrance is a description of how the store operates. You may visit the store ONLY ONCE!

There are six floors and the attributes of the men increase as the shopper ascends the flights. There is, however, a catch . . . You may choose any man from a particular floor, or you may choose to go up a floor, but you cannot go back down except to exit the building! So, a woman goes to the Husband Store to find a husband.

On the first floor the sign on the door reads:

Floor 1 - These men have good jobs and love the Lord.

The second floor sign reads:

Floor 2 - These men have good jobs, love the Lord, and love kids.

The third floor sign reads:

Floor 3 - These men have good jobs, love the Lord, they love kids, are very rich and extremely good-looking.

"Wow," she thinks, but feels compelled to keep going. She goes to the fourth floor and sign reads:

 The fourth floor sign reads:

Floor 4 - These men have good jobs, love the Lord, love kids, are very rich, good- looking and help with the housework.

"Oh my God" she exclaimed, "I can hardly stand it!" Still, she goes to the fifth floor and sign reads:

Floor 5 - These men have good jobs, love the Lord, love kids, are very rich, gorgeous, help with the housework, and have a strong romantic streak. She is so tempted to stay, but she goes to the sixth floor and the sign reads:

Floor 6 - You are visitor' number 4,363,012 to this floor. There are no men on this floor. This floor exists solely as proof that women are impossible to please. Thank you for shopping at the Husband Store. Watch your step as you exit the building, and have a nice day!

Please send this to all men for a good laugh and to all the women who can handle the truth!

THE OBEDIENT WIFE

There was a man who had worked hard all his life, had saved all his money, and was a real miser when it came to his money.

Just before he died, he said to his wife…..'When I die, I want you to take all my money and put it in the casket with me. I want to take my money to the afterlife with me.'

And so he got his wife to promise him with all of her heart, that when he died, she would put all of the money into the casket with him.

Well, he died. He was stretched out in the casket, his wife was sitting there – dressed in black, and her friend was sitting next to her.

When they finished the ceremony and just before the undertakers got ready to close the casket, the wife said, 'Wait for just a moment!'

She had a small metal box with her; she came over with the box and put it in the casket.

Then the undertakers locked the casket down and they rolled it away.

So her friend said, "Girl, I know you were not foolish enough to put all that money in there with your husband."

The loyal wife replied, 'Listen, I am a Christian; I cannot go back on my word. I promised him that I was going to put that money into the casket with Him.'

'You mean to tell me you put that money in that casket with him!?!?!?' "I sure did," said the wife. "I got it all together, put it into my account, and wrote him a cheque…….if he can cash it, then he can spend it."

Send this to every clever female you know, and to every man who thinks they are smarter than women!!!

SHAKE THEM HATERS OFF!

A hater is someone that is jealous and envious and spends all their time trying to make you look small so they can look tall. They are very negative people.

Nothing is ever good enough! When you make your mark, you will always attract some haters... That's why you have to be careful who you share your blessings and your dreams with because some folk can't handle seeing you blessed... It's dangerous to be like somebody else... If God wanted you to be like somebody else. He would have given you what He gave them. You don't know what people have gone through to get what they have... The problem I have with haters is that they see my glory, but they don't know my story...

If the grass looks greener on the other side of the fence, you can rest assured that the water bill is higher there too. We've all got some haters among us: Some people don't like it that you can:

* Have a relationship with God

* Light up a room when you walk in

* Start your own business

* Tell a man/woman to get lost (if he/she isn't about the right thing)

* Raise children without both parents being around

* And not ask for a dime from anyone

* Haters don't want to see you happy

* Haters don't want to see you succeed

* Haters don't want you to get the victory

Most of our haters are people that are supposed to be on our side. How do you handle the haters who you at least expect to have your guard up against?

You can handle your haters by:

1. *Knowing who you are and who your true friends are * (VERY IMPORTANT!!)

2. *Having a purpose to your life *

3. *By remembering what you have is by divine prerogative and not human manipulation.*

Purpose does not mean having a job. You can have a job and still be unfulfilled. A purpose is having a clear sense of what God has called you to be. Your purpose is not defined by what others think about you. Fulfil your dreams! You only have one life to live................when it's your time to leave this earth, you want to be able to say, "I've lived my life and fulfilled my dreams. I'm ready to go HOME!

When God gives you a favour, you can tell your haters, "Don't look at me... Look at who is in charge of me..."

FUNNY QUOTES:

Marriage is the next thing to heaven on earth or a hellish experience of life imprisonment with hard labour here on earth.

Marriage is an adventure, like going to war.

Marriage is a wonderful invention: then again, so is a bicycle repair kit.

Marriage is like a phone call in the night: first the ring, and then you wake up

My wife suggested a book for me to read to enhance our relationship. It's titled, "Women are from Venus, Men are Wrong."

When a man steals your wife there is no better revenge than to let him keep her.

It's a funny thing that when a man hasn't anything on earth to worry about, he goes off and gets married.

Love is blind, marriage is the eye-opener.

I was married by a judge. I should have asked for a jury.

I don't worry about terrorism. I was married for two years

A man in love is incomplete until he is married. Then he's finished.

Before marriage, a man declares that he would lay down his life to serve you; after marriage, he won't even lay down his newspaper to talk to you.

There's a way of transferring funds that is even faster than electronic banking. It's called marriage.

Your marriage is in trouble if your wife says, 'You're only interested in one thing,' and you can't remember what it is.

Marriage is give and take. You'd better give it to her or she'll take it anyway.

You know what I did before I married? Anything I wanted to.

The husband who wants a happy marriage should learn to keep his mouth shut and his cheque book open.

My wife and I were happy for twenty years. Then we met.

We always hold hands. If I let go, she shops.

A man's wife has more power over him than the state has.

In my house I'm the boss, my wife is just the decision maker.

Marriage – a book of which the first chapter is written in poetry and the remaining chapters written in prose.

A bachelor is a man who never makes the same mistake once.

My husband said he needed more space. So I locked him outside.

The only time a woman really succeeds in changing a man is when he's a baby.

I fell in love at first sight… I should have looked twice.

Marriage is the only war in which you sleep with the enemy.

The secret of a happy marriage remains a secret.

Marriage is like a hot bath. Once you get used to it, it's not so hot.

There is no more lovely, friendly and charming relationship, communion or company than a good marriage.

Marriage is nature's way of keeping us from fighting with strangers.

Compromise: An amiable arrangement between husband and wife whereby they agree to let her have her own way.

Marriage is a three ring circus: engagement ring, wedding ring, and suffering.

I've had bad luck with both my wives. The first one left me and the second one didn't.

Some people ask the secret of our long marriage. We take time to go to a restaurant two times a week. A little candlelight dinner, soft music and dancing. She goes Tuesdays, I go Fridays.

The appropriate age for marriage is around eighteen for girls and thirty-seven for men.

Bachelors know more about women than married men; if they didn't, they'd be married too.

I got rid of my husband. The cat was allergic.

I require only three things of a man. He must be handsome, ruthless and stupid.

Keep your eyes wide open before marriage and half-shut afterwards.

I never knew what real happiness was until I got married.

And by then it was too late.

Marriage has no guarantees. If that's what you're looking for, go live with a car battery.

Marriage is a wonderful institution, but who wants to live in an institution?

After marriage, husband and wife become two sides of a coin; they just can't face each other, but still they stay together.

A dress that zips up the back will bring a husband and wife together.
James H. Boren

A good marriage would be between a blind wife and a deaf husband.
Michel de Montaigne

A husband is what is left of a lover, after the nerve has been extracted.
Helen Rowland

A journey is like marriage. The certain way to be wrong is to think you control it.
John Steinbeck

A man in love is incomplete until he has married. Then he's finished.
Zsa Zsa Gabor

A man marries to have a home, but also because he doesn't

want to be bothered with sex and all that sort of thing.
W. Somerset Maugham

A psychiatrist asks a lot of expensive questions your wife asks for nothing.
Joey Adams

A successful marriage requires falling in love many times, always with the same person.
Mignon McLaughlin

A wedding is a funeral where you smell your own flowers.
Eddie Cantor

All marriages are happy. It's the living together afterward that causes all the trouble.
Raymond Hull

All men make mistakes, but married men find out about them sooner.
Red Skelton

Bachelors have consciences, married men have wives.
Samuel Johnson

Almost no one is foolish enough to imagine that he automatically deserves great success in any field of activity; yet almost everyone believes that he automatically deserves success in marriage.
Sydney J. Harris

An ideal wife is one who remains faithful to you but tries to be just as charming as if she weren't.
Sacha Guitry

Any intelligent woman who reads the marriage contract, and then goes into it, deserves all the consequences.
Isadora Duncan

Bachelors know more about women than married men; if they didn't they'd be married too.
H. L. Mencken

Basically my wife was immature. I'd be at home in the bath and she'd come in and sink my boats.
Woody Allen

Before marriage, a girl has to make love to a man to hold him. After marriage, she has to hold him to make love to him.
Marilyn Monroe

Being divorced is like being hit by a Mack truck. If you live through it, you start looking very carefully to the right and to the left.
Jean Kerr

But, alas! What poor Woman is ever taught that she should have a higher Design than to get her a Husband?

Read more: http://www.brainyquote.com/quotes/topics/topic_marriage.html#ixzz1MiyvbBIe

NOTES:

THE GREATEST GIFT

If you want to take advantage of the contents of this message by asking God to give you power to lead, from which Adam fell, you need to give your life to Jesus Christ. If you have never met or experienced a definite encounter with Jesus Christ, you can know Him today. You can make your life right with Him by accepting Him as your personal Lord and Saviour by praying the following prayer out loud where you are. Pray this prayer with me now:

PRAYER FOR SALVATION: 'O God, I ask you to forgive me for my sins. I believe You sent Jesus to die on the cross for me and confess it with my mouth. I receive Jesus Christ as my personal Lord and Saviour and confess Him as Lord of my life and I give my life willingly to Him now. Thank you Lord for saving me and for making me a new person in Jesus' Name, (2 Corinthians 5:17) Amen.'

If you prayed this prayer, you have now become a child of God (John 1:12) and I welcome you to the family of God. Please let me know about your decision for Jesus by writing to me. I would like to send you some free literature to help you in your new walk with the Lord. So please write to me at the following address:

Correspondence address:

Michael Hutton-Wood,

House of Judah (Praise) Ministries

P. O. Box 1226,

Croydon. CR9 6DG. UK.

Or call:

Within the UK:

0208 689 6010, 07956 815 714

Outside the UK:

+44 208 689 6010, +44 7956 815 714

Alternatively Email us at:

Email: info@houseofjudah.org.uk

michaelhutton-wood@fsmail.net

Or visit us at: Website: www.houseofjudah.org.uk

Watch our 24hour internet TV experience on www.judahtv.org

OTHER BOOKS AND LEADERSHIP MANUALS BY AUTHOR

1. A Must For Every New Convert
2. You Need To Do The Ridiculous In Order To Experience The Miraculous
3. 175 Reasons Why You Cannot And Will Not Fail In Life
4. What To Do In The Darkest Hour Of Your Trial [125 Bible Truths You Must Know, BELIEVE, REMEMBER, CONFESS AND DO]
5. Why You should Pray And How You should Pray For Your Pastor and Your Church Daily
6. 200 Questions You Must Ask, Investigate And Know Before You Say 'I Do'
7. I Shall Rise Again
8. How to negotiate your desired future with today's currency
9. Leadership Secrets
10. Leadership Nuggets
11. Leadership Capsules
12. Success is by choice and failure is by choice
13. The Dangers of Procrastination
14. Wisdom Bank

Training Manuals For Impactful Leadership & Effective Ministry

Academy 101 [House Of Judah Academy Curriculum]

Ministry 101

Leadership 101

Kingdom Prosperity 101 From School Of Kingdom Prosperity & Financial Management

Pastoral Leadership 101 From School Of Impactful Pastoral Leadership

Prescriptions For Fulfilling Your Ministry

To order copies of any of these books, ministry or leadership manuals or for a product catalog of other literature, audiotapes and CDs, DVDs, write to:

Michael Hutton-Wood Ministries, P. O. Box 1226, Croydon. CR9 6DG. UK. or [in the UK call] - 0208 689 6010; [outside UK call] + 442086896010

You can also place your order online as you visit our website: www.houseofjudah.org.uk

You can also email us at: Email: info@houseofjudah.org.uk; or michaelhutton-wood@fsmail.net

Global Initiatives And Ministries Within The Ministry

TV MINISTRY IN THE UK
Watch Leadership Secrets on KICC TV
SKY Channel 594

Tuesday & Thursday – 3pm & Saturday 5.30pm

Monday-Friday 2pm on FAITH TV
Sky channel 593 & Saturday 3.30pm

LOG ON AND WATCH OUR INTERNET TV PROGRAM on WWW.JUDAHTV.ORG

Anytime - anywhere.

Featuring the:
Teaching Channel
Motivation Channel
Leadership Channel
Family/ Relationships Channel
Upcoming Events/ Products

WATCH US ON YouTube and AUDIO STREAMING EVERY WEEK @ www.houseofjudah.org.uk

Partnering With A Global Ministry Within A Ministry

Michael Hutton-Wood Ministries (The HUTTON-WOOD WORLD OUTREACH MINISTRY) is the apostolic, missions, world outreach, and evangelistic wing of the House of Judah (Praise) Ministries with a mission to God's end time church and the nations of the earth. This ministry was born out of a strong God-given mandate to reach, touch and impact the nations of the earth with the gospel of Christ and bring back divine order, discipline, integrity, godly character, excellence and stability to God's people and God's house. It has a strong apostolic mandate to set in order the things that are out of order and lacking in the church [The Body of Christ] – (Titus 1:5).

Its mission is to save the lost at any cost, depopulate hell and populate heaven with souls that have experienced in full, the new birth, renewal of mind, to produce believers walking in the fullness of their Godly inheritance, divine health, prosperity and authority to take their homes, communities, cities and nations for Christ and occupy till Christ returns. It is to raise a people without spot, wrinkle or blemish. The man of God's passion and drive is that as truly as he lives, this earth shall be filled with the knowledge of the glory of the Lord as the waters cover the sea. His determination is not to rest, hold back or keep silent until he sees the body of Christ established as a praise in the earth. (Numbers 14:21; Habakkuk 2:14; Isaiah 62:6-7)

If you would like to join the faithful brethren and partners of this great ministry by becoming a partner as we believe God for ten thousand partners to partner with this vision prayerfully and financially, ask for a copy of the partners' club commitment card by writing to:

Michael Hutton-Wood Ministries

[Hutton-Wood World Outreach]

P. O. Box 1226, Croydon. Surrey.

CR9 6DG. UK.

Alternatively, you can send a monthly contribution by cheque payable to our ministry or donate online at www.houseofjudah.org.uk or request a direct debit mandate or standing order form from your bankers or us made payable to Michael Hutton-Wood Ministries. Call +44 [0] 208 689 6010 for more details. Philippians 4:19 be your portion and experience as you partner with this work and global mandate. Shalom!

Generational Leadership Training Institute

(The Leaders' Factory)

The Mandate: Raising Generational Leaders, Impacting Nations.

The Generational Leadership Training Institute (GLTI) is the Leadership training and mentoring wing of our ministry with a global mandate to raise leaders with a generational thinking mindset, not a now mentality and to fulfil the Law of Explosive Growth – To add growth, lead followers – To multiply, lead leaders.

This is a Bible College, Leadership Training Institute fulfilling the Matthew 9:37-38 mandate of developing and releasing labourers for the end time harvest. We offer fulltime and part time certificate, diploma, degree and short twelve-week courses in biblical studies, counselling, leadership, practical ministry and schools of prosperity. Its aim is to raise leaders who know and live not just by the anointing but by ministerial ethics, leaders who build with a long term mentality, who live today with tomorrow in mind. The mission of this unique educational and impartation institution is to transform followers into generational leaders and its motto is to raise leaders of discipline, integrity, godly character and excellence - D.I.C.E.

For correspondence, full time, part time, online courses,

prospectus, fees and registration forms for the next course, call 0208 689 6010 or write to the Registrar, GLTI, P. O. Box 1226, Croydon. CR9 6DG. UK or from outside UK call +44 208 689 6010.

Additional information can be obtained from visiting our website www.houseofjudah.org.uk looking for THE LEADERS FACTORY.

Log on to www.judahtv.org for Leadership Secrets and other teaching.

This is a hutton-wood publication

LEADERS FACTORY INTERNATIONAL

MANDATE: 'In the business of training, developing and raising and releasing more leaders and leaders of leaders.'

'Leaders must be close enough to relate to others, but far enough ahead to motivate them.' – John Maxwell

'You must live with people to know their problems, and live with God in order to solve them.' – P. T. Forsyth

If you, your organisation, college, university, business or church would like to invite Dr. Michael Hutton-Wood for a Motivational-speaking, mentoring or leadership coaching engagement or to organize or hold a Leaders Factory seminar or conference, Leadership Development or Human Capital building seminar, Emerging leaders seminar, Management seminar, Business seminar, Effective people-management, Wealth-creation seminar or training for your workers, leaders, staff, ministers, employers, employees, congregation, youth, etc. you can contact us on 0208 689 6010 [UK] +44208 689 6010 [OUTSIDE UK].

Alternatively by email at:

- info@houseofjudah.org.uk

- michaelhutton-wood@fsmail.net

or leadersfactoryinternational@yahoo.com

VISIT our website: www.houseofjudah.org.uk

You can watch our internet TV experience www.judahtv.org [Maximizing Destiny and Leadership Secrets].

This is a Hutton-Wood publication

MANDATE:

Releasing Potential - Maximizing Destiny

Raising Generational Leaders - Impacting Nations

SIMPA

SCEPTRE INTERNATIONAL MINISTERS & PASTORS ASSOCIATION

This covenant mandate comes from Genesis 49:10: 'The sceptre [of Leadership] shall not depart from JUDAH, nor a lawgiver from between his feet, until Shiloh come and unto Him shall the gathering of the people be'

Other covenant scriptures backing this mandate are: Isaiah 55:4 & Titus 1:5. We have a leadership assignment to RAISE GENERATIONAL LEADERS TO IMPACT NATIONS BY DISCOVERING MEN/WOMEN AND EMPOWERING THEM TO RELEASE THEIR POTENTIAL TO MAXIMIZE THEIR DESTINY.

SIMPA is a multi-cultural fellowship/network of diverse Christian leaders, pastors and ministers that recognize the need for fathering, covering and mentoring. The heartbeat of the man of God is to pour into the willing and obedient what has made him and keeps making him from what he's learnt from his father in the Lord, his teachers and mentors which is working for him and producing maximally. He said: 'I discovered this secret early: Not to learn from or follow those who make promises but from those who have obtained the promises, proofs and results. REMEMBER: YOU

DON'T NEED TO MAKE NOISE TO MAKE NEWS. SO: FOLLOW NEWS-MAKERS NOT NOISE-MAKERS!'

These are a few of the mindsets of the man of God:

When the students are ready, the teacher will teach.

'YOU NEED FATHERS TO FATHER YOU TO GROW FEATHERS TO FLY.' – Bishop Oyedepo

'Without a father to father you, you can never grow feathers to fly and go further in life, than they went and accomplish more than they did.' – Michael Hutton-Wood

Don't raise money; raise men and you'll have all the money you need to accomplish your assignment.

There is no new thing under the sun – King Solomon

What you desire to attain, become and accomplish in life, someone has accomplished it – find them, follow them, learn from them, sow into them and their resource materials and you will do more than they did and get there faster.

Teachers, Trainers, Mentors and Fathers give you speed/acceleration in every field of endeavour.

Isaac Newton is known to have said the following:

'If I have seen further it has been by standing on the shoulders of those who have gone ahead of me.'

Variant translations: 'Plato is my friend, Aristotle is my friend, but my best friend is truth.'

'Plato is my friend — Aristotle is my friend — truth is a

greater friend.'

'If I have seen further it is only by standing on the shoulders of giants.'

Without a reference you can never become a reference.

If you don't refer to anyone no one will refer to you.

Who laid / lays hands on you and what did / do they leave behind?

This is not a money-making venture but rather about covering and empowerment for fulfilment of destiny and assignment within time allocated.

The goal of SIMPA is to spiritually cover, strengthen, equip, empower, train, mentor and encourage and lift up the arms/hands of both emerging and active [full and part time] pastors, ministers and leaders and by so doing release them to fulfil their respective assignments both in ministry and the market place.

IF YOU WOULD LIKE TO BE A PART OF SIMPA, ASK FOR A REGISTRATION FORM & PAMPHLET FROM OUR INFORMATION DESK in House of Judah or email info@houseofjudah.org.uk or call [in the UK] 0208 689 6010 [outside UK call] + 44 208 689 6010 requesting for SIMPA registration form and pamphlet.

– SEE YOU ON TOP!

Shalom! – Bishop

PARTNERSHIP:

In the UK write or send cheque donations to:
Michael Hutton-Wood Ministries
P. O. Box 1226
Croydon. CR9 6DG. UK.

In the UK Call: 0208 689 6010; 07956 815 714
Outside the UK call: +44 208 689 6010;
+ 44 7956 815 714
Fax: +44 20 8689 3301
Email:
info@houseofjudah.org.uk
michaelhutton-wood@fsmail.net
leadersfactoryinternational@yahoo.com
judah@houseofjudah.freeserve.co.uk

Or visit or donate online at our secure
WEBSITE: www.houseofjudah.org.uk

Watch our 24 hour internet TV experience by logging on anywhere - anytime @ www.judahtv.org

BOOKS AND LEADERSHIP MANUALS
BY BISHOP MICHAEL HUTTON-WOOD

What is Ministry

My Daily Bible Reading Guide

Leadership Nuggets

175 Reasons Why You Cannot And Will Not Fail In Life

I Shall Rise Agian

Leadership Capsules

What To Do In The Darkest Hour of Your Trial

Generating Finances For Ministry

TRAINING MANUALS FOR IMPACTFUL LEADERSHIP & EFFECTIVE MINISTRY

Please log on to **www.houseofjudah.org.uk** for more information

OTHER BOOKS BY THE AUTHOR
- BISHOP MICHAEL HUTTON-WOOD -

Why You Should Pray for your Pastor And For Your Church Daily

200 Questions You Must Ask, Investigate And Know Before You Say I Do

A Must For Every New Convert

How To Negotiate Your Desired Future With Today's Currency

Leadership Secrets

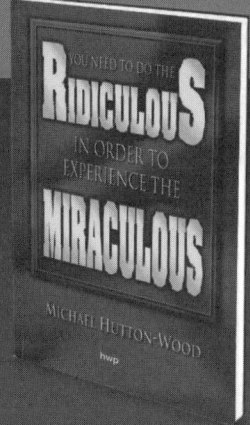

You Need To Do The Ridiculous In Order To Experience The Miraculous

Please log on to
www.houseofjudah.org.uk for more information